Second Shot, Better Aim

Reinventing Work After 50 - A practical and inspiring roadmap for professionals over 50 to redefine their career path, build meaningful work, and thrive in the second half of life with sharper focus and renewed purpose

Nicci Brochard
&
Dr. Ben Chuba

Second Shot, Better Aim

Reinventing Work After 50 - A practical and inspiring roadmap for professionals over 50 to redefine their career path, build meaningful work, and thrive in the second half of life with sharper focus and renewed purpose

CROSSBORDER

New York, London, Quebec

Contents

Introduction

Welcome. Here to our ever-evolving world; the notion of career advancement and fulfillment often seems reserved for the young. But for those over the age of 50, the second half of life offers a unique opportunity to redefine what work means and how it can serve a person's passions, purpose, and goals. "Second Shot, Better Aim" isn't just another career development book—it's a call to action for seasoned professionals to leverage their wisdom, experience, and skills to chart a new, fulfilling career path. This roadmap is designed to inspire and empower individuals over 50 to not just adapt to the future of work but to seize it with confidence, creativity, and focus.

For many, turning 50 can feel like a crossroads, a point where both possibilities and challenges coexist. While some might feel the weight of age-related stereotypes or the fear of becoming irrelevant in a youth-dominated job market, "Second Shot, Better Aim" shows that this is the prime time to embrace a fresh perspective and pursue meaningful work that aligns with your values, aspirations, and life's purpose. The journey to reinvention may seem daunting, but with the right tools, mindset, and a clear vision, professionals can enter the second half of their careers with renewed vigor and excitement.

This book outlines a practical and empowering framework for navigating the complexities of reinvention in the workplace after 50. It

1

provides a clear pathway for those seeking to transition into new fields, refine their current roles, or launch entrepreneurial ventures with greater purpose and fulfillment. Whether you're a corporate veteran, a small business owner, or someone considering a complete career pivot, "Second Shot, Better Aim" offers guidance on how to take your valuable skillset and apply it in ways that are both meaningful and rewarding.

At the heart of this journey is the idea that experience is not a limitation but a treasure trove of insights and capabilities that younger generations simply haven't had the chance to acquire yet. After decades of honing professional expertise, those over 50 possess a wealth of knowledge that can be transformative in the workplace. From leadership skills to problem-solving abilities, their accumulated wisdom makes them invaluable assets, capable of bringing a fresh and seasoned perspective to the table.

But success doesn't come automatically—it requires intentional action. "Second Shot, Better Aim" provides readers with the tools to sharpen their focus and revitalize their careers. It includes practical advice on updating skill sets for the modern job market, building a personal brand that resonates with today's employers, and making a lasting impact in any career, whether through nonprofit work, consulting, teaching, or innovation within a current role.

Moreover, this book emphasizes the importance of mindset in the reinvention process. It challenges limiting beliefs and urges readers to view the second half of their careers not as a decline, but as an opportunity for growth, contribution, and self-discovery. Through inspiring real-life stories, actionable strategies, and a step-by-step approach, "Second Shot, Better Aim" guides you through the transformation from uncertainty to clarity, from stagnation to excitement, and from fear to action.

As you read, you will be encouraged to examine your passions, goals, and strengths through a new lens. You'll be asked to reflect on what truly matters to you—what you want your legacy to be, and how you can align your work with your purpose. With a clearer vision and a sense of renewed energy, this book offers you a practical guide to take that second shot, armed with the insight, confidence, and sharper aim necessary to make the second half of your career the best half yet.

"Second Shot, Better Aim" isn't about retiring from the world of work—it's about reinvention. It's about taking all the lessons, experiences, and skills you've gathered over the years and using them to create a life of work that excites you, challenges you, and allows you to thrive with a renewed sense of purpose. Your second shot is waiting. It's time to take aim and build the career you've always dreamed of.

Nicci and I (Ben) thank you immensely for choosing our book. We promise you a great time ahead.

Chapter 1

The Second Act is Calling

Why 50 Isn't the End—It's a Smarter Beginning

The age of 50 can often feel like a precipice, a moment when many people start to reflect on what they have accomplished and what remains to be done. The thought of leaving behind a well-trodden career path can seem daunting, even impossible. But for many, 50 is not the end—it's just the beginning of a new, smarter act in life and work. This chapter explores why the second act is not just a possibility but an exciting opportunity for reinvention, growth, and purpose.

Busting Myths About Aging and Careers

Let's start by addressing a critical issue head-on: the myths and misconceptions that surround aging and career changes. Society often casts a long shadow on individuals over 50, making them believe that their careers are winding down, or worse, over. These myths, deeply ingrained in cultural attitudes, have caused many to feel sidelined as they approach the second half of their lives. But the truth is, these assumptions are often based on outdated ideas about aging and work.

One of the most pervasive myths is the idea that it's too late to learn new skills. The narrative often goes like this: "By 50, you're set in your ways, and it's impossible to reinvent yourself." However, the reality is much different. As people age, they accumulate a vast wealth of experience that helps them adapt more quickly to new challenges. Research consistently shows that learning capacity doesn't significantly decline with age; instead, it shifts. The brain's neuroplasticity allows older adults to acquire new skills and adapt to new environments, provided they maintain a growth mindset. The key is being open to learning and staying curious.

Another common myth is that older workers are less productive or less flexible than their younger counterparts. This myth is tied to the assumption that youth equals energy and drive. While it's true that physical energy might decline as we age, productivity is not solely reliant on physical stamina. In fact, older workers often bring invaluable qualities to the workplace, including a high degree of emotional intelligence, a strong work ethic, and a wealth of problem-solving experience. They are more likely to approach work strategically, using their experience to avoid common pitfalls and deliver results more efficiently.

The notion that career change is only for the young is also misguided. The reality is that career reinvention after 50 is not only possible, but many people thrive in their second acts. In fact, older workers often bring a fresh perspective to industries and roles that younger workers might overlook. Many industries, such as technology and entrepreneurship, are experiencing a wave of older professionals who have chosen to pivot into new fields, bringing their expertise, life experience, and problem-solving skills with them.

Moreover, the traditional "linear" career path—progressing from one role to the next, following a prescribed trajectory—has become less relevant in today's world of work. The gig economy, remote work, freelancing, and entrepreneurial ventures have opened up new pathways for people at any stage of their careers to reinvent themselves and craft meaningful work that aligns with their values and passions.

Real-Life Stories of Late Bloomers and Second-Act Successes

To truly understand the potential of a second act, it's important to look at the real-life stories of individuals who embraced change later in life. These stories aren't just inspirational—they provide concrete examples of how it's possible to build something new and exciting at any age.

Take the story of Julia Child, the beloved chef and television personality. Child didn't start her culinary career until she was in her 40s. Before that, she had worked as a secretary and in various administrative roles. But it wasn't until she moved to France and discovered her passion for cooking that her true career began. Her cookbook, *Mastering the Art of French Cooking*, was published when she was 50, and her TV show followed shortly after. Julia Child's story is a testament to the fact that a second act can be even more fulfilling than the first.

Another powerful example is Ray Kroc, who is often credited with turning McDonald's into the global fast-food empire it is today. Kroc was 52 years old when he took the helm of McDonald's, a company that had already been founded by Richard and Maurice McDonald. Prior to this,

Kroc had worked in various jobs, including as a milkshake machine salesman. It wasn't until his early 50s that he decided to invest in the McDonald brothers' business. His decision to buy the company and expand it changed not only the fast-food industry but the entire global business landscape.

Then there's Vera Wang, the famous fashion designer who was a figure skater and journalist before entering the fashion industry. Wang didn't design her first wedding dress until she was 40 years old, and she didn't open her first bridal boutique until she was 41. Today, she is one of the most influential designers in the world, revolutionizing the wedding industry.

These examples show that reinvention is not just a theoretical idea— it's a proven reality for countless individuals. The idea that a fulfilling career has an expiration date is patently false. Instead, 50 can be the launchpad for your greatest professional accomplishments yet.

The Emotional and Psychological Triggers Behind Career Reinvention

As with any major life transition, the decision to reinvent oneself after 50 often comes with emotional and psychological hurdles. These barriers can feel especially daunting because they involve both internal and external forces. Internally, individuals may struggle with self-doubt, fear of failure, or anxiety about the unknown. Externally, societal expectations and stereotypes about aging can create pressure and make it seem like a career shift is impossible.

One of the most significant emotional triggers is the fear of starting over. Many people over 50 have invested decades of time and energy into building their careers, and the thought of starting from scratch can feel overwhelming. It's important to acknowledge that feeling this way is natural, but it's also crucial to remember that a career reinvention doesn't have to mean starting from the very bottom. Your experience, skills, and expertise are valuable assets that you carry with you, and they can be leveraged in new ways. Reinvention doesn't require abandoning everything—it's about adapting and finding new opportunities within your existing knowledge and abilities.

Another psychological trigger is the fear of not being taken seriously. Age discrimination remains a reality in many industries, and individuals over 50 often worry that potential employers or business partners will view them as "too old" or "out of touch." Combatting this fear requires a shift in mindset. The truth is, your experience is an asset, not a liability. Emphasizing how your background can bring a fresh perspective to an organization is key to overcoming this fear. For many, embracing their experience and presenting it as an advantage is the first step in dispelling doubts about their capabilities.

A significant psychological hurdle for many individuals in their 50s is the idea that it's "too late" to reinvent themselves. However, research shows that people in midlife often experience a renewed sense of purpose and clarity, allowing them to make more deliberate and meaningful career decisions. The second act is an opportunity to work with a deeper sense of purpose, to choose endeavors that align with personal values, and to pursue a career that feels more authentic and fulfilling.

Additionally, this age marks a period of reflection and a reassessment of life goals. People in their 50s often find themselves asking, "What is truly important to me? What do I want to accomplish before I retire?" These questions can serve as powerful motivators, driving people to pursue passions they may have put off for years. This is where the emotional and psychological triggers of career reinvention become an opportunity for personal growth and transformation.

How Work Purpose Evolves After Midlife

For many individuals over 50, the purpose of work begins to shift. No longer is career success defined solely by titles, salary, or traditional markers of achievement. Instead, it becomes more about finding work that aligns with personal values, contributes to a larger community, and provides fulfillment on a deeper level.

In the first half of life, many people focus on climbing the career ladder—seeking promotions, raises, and recognition. But as individuals approach their 50s, they often begin to reconsider what truly drives them. What was once a singular focus on financial gain or prestige evolves into a desire for meaningful contributions and work that aligns with one's passions and values. It's a time when people start thinking about their legacy—what they want to leave behind, both in terms of their work and their impact on the world.

Work purpose in midlife also reflects a desire for more balance. Many people who have spent years working long hours in high-stress jobs seek careers that offer greater flexibility and personal fulfillment. This shift can be particularly liberating for those who have grown tired of the corporate grind and are ready to pursue work that allows them to have a deeper connection to their communities or make a more significant difference in the world.

For some, this means returning to education or teaching, mentoring younger generations, or starting a business that aligns with their personal passions. For others, it might involve taking on consulting roles or participating in non-profit work. The second act is an opportunity to ask deeper questions about one's legacy, personal goals, and desires for work-life harmony. This evolution of work purpose is both liberating and empowering, enabling individuals to design careers that offer not just financial security, but also a sense of satisfaction and alignment with their core values.

The second act in life offers a smarter beginning, not an end. It's an invitation to embrace reinvention, challenge the myths of aging, and recognize that purpose and fulfillment can evolve well beyond 50. By embracing the opportunities for career reinvention, tapping into the wisdom gained over a lifetime, and using the second act as an opportunity to redefine work, individuals can build careers that are not just successful but meaningful. This is the beginning of something far more exciting and transformative than the end of anything.

Conclusion: As you begin to embrace the notion of your second act, it's important to shift your mindset. Fifty is not the end of the road—far from it. It's a new beginning, a smarter and more purposeful starting point where you can harness the power of experience, resilience, and wisdom to reinvent your career. The myths surrounding aging and careers can be debunked with the understanding that career reinvention is not just possible—it's incredibly empowering. Real-life examples of late bloomers and second-act successes, such as Julia Child, Ray Kroc, and Vera Wang, serve as compelling proof that age is not a barrier but a catalyst for reinvention.

In this chapter, you've learned how to overcome the emotional and psychological triggers that come with making a career change later in life. The key lies in shifting from a mindset of limitation to one of possibility, and embracing the second act as an exciting opportunity. The purpose of work evolves with age, and midlife offers a unique chance to align your career with deeper values and passions. Now, armed with the understanding that this new phase is about growth, self-fulfillment, and contribution, you are ready to take your first step into this exciting new chapter.

Chapter 2

Inventorying You—Skills, Wisdom, and Hidden Assets

You're More Than Your Job Title

The notion of career reinvention doesn't begin with searching for the next job or business opportunity. It begins with a deep and honest inventory of who you are, what you've accomplished, and what you have to offer. After 50, it's easy to become defined by your job title or the role you've occupied for years, but in reality, you are far more than the job you held, the company you worked for, or the projects you completed. This chapter is about understanding that you are not defined by just your role—you are the culmination of skills, experiences, relationships, and insights that form a unique set of assets. To reinvent your career effectively, you need to first understand and inventory these assets.

The process of inventorying yourself is both introspective and strategic. It's about identifying not just the hard skills you've accumulated, but also the "soft assets" that make you a valuable professional and individual. These hidden assets, often undervalued by traditional job markets, are what give you the depth and resilience to thrive in new environments. It's important to remember that at 50, you're not starting from scratch; you're starting with a wealth of untapped potential, both tangible and intangible.

How to Audit Your Career Skills, Passions, and Transferable Experience

When considering a career shift or reinvention, the first step is to conduct a thorough audit of your skills, experiences, and passions. Start by listing the key competencies and technical skills that you have gained throughout your career. These may include specialized knowledge, certifications, or expertise in particular areas. For example, if you've spent years in marketing, your technical skills might include campaign management, SEO, content creation, and social media strategy. If you have a background in project management, your technical expertise might involve budgeting, team coordination, and schedule management.

However, a true career audit doesn't stop at these core technical skills. The next crucial step is to identify your transferable experience—those abilities and knowledge that can be applied to different industries or roles. Perhaps your ability to manage a team is as valuable in one industry as it is in another. Or maybe your experience with client relations translates well into a consulting role. The key is to look beyond your specific job function and consider how your expertise can serve a variety of contexts.

For instance, a lawyer who has worked in corporate law may find that their skills in negotiation, analysis, and legal strategy are highly transferable to a career in business consulting or in a non-profit organization. Similarly, someone who has spent years in sales may discover that their skills in client engagement, relationship-building, and persuasion are valuable in fields as diverse as marketing, education, and customer experience.

Identifying Undervalued "Soft Assets" Like Leadership, Resilience, and People Skills

While hard skills are essential, they are only part of the equation when it comes to career reinvention. Often, the most significant assets that professionals over 50 bring to the table are not technical but interpersonal. These soft assets are frequently undervalued in job descriptions and can be overlooked by both job seekers and employers, but they are incredibly powerful. Leadership, resilience, emotional intelligence, and people skills are among the most valuable qualities a professional can possess.

Leadership is one such asset. Over the years, you have likely gained a wealth of experience in leading teams, mentoring junior staff, and managing difficult situations. You have developed the ability to make decisions, motivate others, and set a course for success even in challenging circumstances. These leadership qualities are crucial for any organization or role, whether you are in charge of a team, running a small business, or taking on a consulting project.

Resilience is another often-overlooked quality. In any career, there are inevitable setbacks—failed projects, layoffs, economic downturns, and personal challenges. Over the course of your career, you have built the mental and emotional fortitude to keep going, adapt to changing circumstances, and bounce back from failure. Resilience is what allows

14

you to thrive when faced with adversity, and it is a trait that only deepens with age and experience.

Emotional intelligence (EQ) is also a crucial soft skill, especially in today's interconnected, diverse work environments. Emotional intelligence involves the ability to understand and manage your own emotions while empathizing with others. It's the ability to read social cues, resolve conflicts, and build strong relationships. This is an asset that becomes more refined with age. As you've gained experience in various professional and personal situations, your EQ has likely grown, making you a more effective communicator and a more trusted collaborator.

Finally, don't overlook the value of your communication and people skills. The ability to interact with others in a way that fosters collaboration, motivates, and persuades is one of the most valuable assets you can possess. Whether through written communication, presentations, or face-to-face conversations, your ability to engage and connect with others is something that grows stronger with age.

These soft assets might be harder to quantify than technical skills, but they often make the difference between success and failure in a given role. They are the intangible qualities that will serve you well in a second act, particularly in leadership positions, consulting, or entrepreneurial ventures where people skills and emotional intelligence are critical.

The Hidden Power of Your Network and Reputation

As you inventory your career assets, don't forget the enormous value of your network and reputation. After decades of work, you likely have a network that spans industries, roles, and geographical locations. This network is not just a collection of contacts; it's an invaluable resource that can open doors, provide opportunities, and offer advice as you pursue your second act.

The strength of your network lies in the relationships you've built over the years. These relationships are often deeply rooted in trust, mutual respect, and shared experiences. When you start considering a new career direction or entrepreneurial venture, your network is the first place to look for support, guidance, and even partnerships. People in your network know you, trust you, and are more likely to refer you to opportunities or offer you advice when you need it.

Your reputation is equally important. Over the years, you've established a track record of reliability, expertise, and professional integrity. In many ways, your reputation precedes you, and it can open doors or serve as a solid foundation when you decide to transition into something new. If you've built a strong reputation for being a leader, a problem solver, or an innovator, those qualities will continue to serve you, even in your second act.

The reputation you've cultivated also plays a critical role in shaping your personal brand. As you embark on a new career direction, your reputation can help position you as a thought leader or expert in your field. The connections you've made, the achievements you've accumulated, and the goodwill you've generated all contribute to how you're perceived by others.

Tools: Personal Asset Worksheet & Skill-Mapping Matrix

To help you get started on auditing your career assets, here are two practical tools to guide you through the process: the Personal Asset Worksheet and the Skill-Mapping Matrix.

Personal Asset Worksheet

This worksheet will help you inventory your skills, experiences, and hidden assets. Take the time to reflect on your career and document the following:

1. **Hard Skills:**

2. List the technical competencies and specialized knowledge you have acquired over the years. Include certifications, training, and expertise in your industry.

3. **Transferable Skills:**

4.   Identify the skills that can be applied to other industries or roles. Think about problem-solving, project management, leadership, and other abilities that transcend your current role.

5. **Soft Assets:**

6.   Write down the emotional and interpersonal strengths you have developed, such as leadership, resilience, emotional intelligence, communication skills, and teamwork.

7. **Network:**

8. List key individuals in your professional network. Include mentors, colleagues, clients, and anyone else who has supported or collaborated with you over the years.

9. **Reputation & Personal Brand:**

10. Reflect on your professional reputation. What values do people associate with you? What kind of legacy have you built in your career?

Skill-Mapping Matrix

This matrix will help you map your skills to potential career opportunities. Create a grid with the following columns:

1. **Skill/Experience**

2. List your skills and experiences.

3. **Current Role or Industry**

4. Identify how this skill is applied in your current career.

5. **Potential Role/Industry**

6. Think about how this skill can be transferred to a new role or industry. For example, project management skills can be applied in almost any field, from construction to technology to education.

7. **Learning Needs**

8. Are there any gaps in your knowledge or experience that you need to address in order to make the shift? For example, you

might need to learn new software or develop a deeper understanding of a new industry.

These tools will help you conduct a comprehensive audit of your assets and map out your next steps in career reinvention. With a clear understanding of your skills, strengths, and potential, you can move forward with confidence and clarity.

The process of inventorying yourself is about more than just listing your qualifications—it's about recognizing the full range of assets you bring to the table. These assets are not only technical but also emotional, interpersonal, and relational. By recognizing your value beyond your job title, you can unlock a world of opportunities and step into your second act with purpose, passion, and readiness.

Conclusion: The process of inventorying yourself is the critical first step in career reinvention. It's about recognizing that you're not defined by just your job title but by the vast collection of skills, experiences, and personal qualities you've developed over a lifetime. By conducting a thorough audit of your career skills, passions, and transferable experience, you unlock the hidden potential within yourself that may have been overlooked or undervalued.

In this chapter, we've delved into the often-underappreciated "soft assets"—like leadership, resilience, and emotional intelligence—that set you apart from others. These are the qualities that deepen over time and become your greatest assets as you embark on your second act. Furthermore, we explored the hidden power of your network and reputation. The relationships and credibility you've built throughout your career can open doors to new opportunities and provide valuable support during your transition.

By using the tools provided—such as the Personal Asset Worksheet and Skill-Mapping Matrix—you've begun to build a clear, comprehensive picture of your professional value. With this inventory in hand, you now have the clarity and confidence to move forward and embrace new career opportunities that align with your skills, experience, and passions. Remember, you are more than your job title—your true value lies in the full range of assets you bring to the table, and the next chapter of your career is waiting to be written with purpose and intention.

Chapter 3

What Do You Really Want Now?

Aligning Values, Passion, and Lifestyle

The pursuit of career reinvention doesn't just begin with a skillset audit or an analysis of your experience—it also requires a deep exploration of your core desires. After years of career focus, it's easy to lose sight of what truly drives you. The second act of your career offers an extraordinary opportunity to reconnect with your deeper values, passions, and lifestyle aspirations. But before you dive into the logistics of your next career move, you must first ask yourself: *What do you really want now?*

In this chapter, we will explore how to rethink the concept of success, uncover what motivates you at this stage in your life, and learn how to align your career choices with your personal values and passions. This process involves letting go of outdated definitions of success, moving beyond the paycheck, and instead focusing on what genuinely lights you up. You'll learn how to visualize your ideal work/life blend, make decisions with clarity, and approach your second act with a deep sense of purpose and satisfaction.

Rethinking Success: Purpose > Paycheck

For many people, the pursuit of success has traditionally been measured by external markers—status, salary, title, and power. However, as you approach the second half of your life, it's important to rethink these definitions. While a paycheck and financial security are important, they should not be the primary drivers of your career decisions. In fact, once your basic financial needs are met, the pursuit of purpose and fulfillment should take precedence over external accolades or monetary rewards.

Rethinking success is about shifting your focus from achieving what society deems important to defining what is meaningful to *you*. In your second act, you have the opportunity to question what kind of legacy you want to leave and what kind of impact you want to make on the world. Is your goal to contribute to a cause that's dear to you? Do you want to share your knowledge and experiences with others? Or perhaps you want to create something innovative that inspires and impacts future generations? These are the types of questions that will help you align your career with your personal values.

Take, for instance, the story of Patagonia's founder, Yvon Chouinard, who famously redefined success by focusing on environmental stewardship and corporate responsibility over pure profit-making. Patagonia's commitment to sustainability and ethical business practices has become a model for redefining what success looks like in business. Chouinard's philosophy of aligning work with a larger purpose—beyond the paycheck—has not only led to financial success but has also built a company that people trust and admire for its integrity.

As you approach your second act, it's crucial to evaluate whether your previous definitions of success still resonate with who you are today. Are you still driven by a desire for financial wealth, or do you find that impact, creativity, and freedom now hold more weight in your life? Shifting the focus from monetary rewards to purpose-driven work will help you create a career path that is more fulfilling and meaningful.

Exploring What Motivates You Now: Impact, Freedom, Creativity?

After decades of professional experience, your motivations have likely evolved. You may find that your desires for success now center around more intrinsic values such as *impact, freedom*, and *creativity*—things that weren't as central to your earlier career. Understanding these motivations is key to unlocking the next chapter in your career.

Impact:

Many people over 50 feel an increasing desire to make a tangible difference in the world, whether it's through social entrepreneurship, nonprofit work, or advocacy. At this stage, you may be less interested in climbing the corporate ladder or amassing wealth, and more focused on creating a positive, lasting impact on society or the environment. Think about the causes that have always resonated with you, whether it's environmental sustainability, education, or healthcare. Finding a career path that allows you to contribute meaningfully to these causes will provide the kind of fulfillment that traditional success markers can't match.

For example, Malala Yousafzai, after surviving a tragic assassination attempt, turned her attention to advocating for girls' education worldwide. While her experience with the violence was tragic, it fueled her desire to make an impact. This newfound focus on her purpose allowed her to build an incredible platform to address global issues, showing how personal experiences can shape a higher calling later in life.

Freedom:

At this stage, many professionals seek greater autonomy in their work. This desire for freedom might manifest in various ways, such as having more control over your schedule, being able to choose the projects you work on, or even the ability to work from anywhere in the world. Perhaps you've spent years in structured corporate environments and now crave a more flexible work-life balance. Pursuing work that offers this flexibility can lead to greater satisfaction and energy, allowing you to live life on your own terms.

Creativity:

For many, creativity becomes a key motivator after 50. After years of structured work, you may now yearn to express yourself more freely, whether through creative endeavors or entrepreneurial projects. Creativity doesn't just belong in artistic professions; it can be applied to problem-solving, product design, marketing strategies, and even leadership styles. If creativity is something you're passionate about, now is the perfect time to explore ways to integrate it into your career.

Visualizing Your Ideal Work/Life Blend

Visualizing your ideal work/life blend is not just about imagining a perfect job—it's about visualizing the life you want to live and how your career fits into that vision. This step is crucial for finding alignment between your personal goals and your professional aspirations. It's important to step back and ask yourself: *What does my ideal life look like, and how can my career support that?*

Your ideal work/life blend might involve having the freedom to travel, spend more time with loved ones, or pursue personal hobbies. Maybe it involves scaling back your hours to focus on passion projects or even shifting to a more flexible, part-time role. The key is to define what balance looks like for you—then design your next career move around that vision.

To help with this visualization, create a mental picture of your perfect day: What time do you wake up? How do you spend your day? What kinds of activities bring you joy and fulfillment? What type of work makes you feel energized rather than drained? Once you have a clearer picture of your ideal life, you can start to design a career path that supports it. Whether that means shifting to a remote job, becoming a consultant, or starting your own business, you will have a better understanding of what actions to take next.

Values Clarity and "Hell Yes" Decision-Making

When considering career reinvention, it's essential to clarify your values. These values will act as your compass, guiding you through the decision-making process as you explore new opportunities. Identifying what truly matters to you—such as integrity, freedom, creativity, or social impact—helps you make career decisions that align with your authentic self.

The "Hell Yes" decision-making process is a powerful tool for ensuring that every decision you make in this new chapter resonates deeply with your core values. When you're presented with an opportunity, whether it's a job offer, a new business venture, or a career change, ask yourself: *Is this a "hell yes" for me?* If the answer is anything less than a resounding, enthusiastic "yes," it might be a sign to reconsider.

The "Hell Yes" framework allows you to weed out opportunities that don't serve your long-term vision, enabling you to make decisions with confidence and clarity. It's a reminder that this second act is yours to design, and it should align fully with the things that matter most to you.

Conclusion

The process of aligning your career with your values, passions, and lifestyle aspirations is key to crafting a fulfilling and meaningful second act. Rethinking success and shifting your focus from paycheck to purpose opens up a world of possibilities. By understanding what motivates you now—whether it's impact, freedom, or creativity—you can better identify the opportunities that will fuel your passion. Visualizing your ideal work/life blend ensures that you create a life that feels balanced and fulfilling. Finally, values clarity and using the "Hell Yes" decision-making process will help you move forward with confidence, knowing that each choice you make is aligned with your authentic self. The second act is your chance to design a career that's not just about work, but about living with purpose, intention, and joy.

Chapter 4

The Career Graveyard—What to Leave Behind

Unlearning Old Scripts and Outdated Beliefs

Introduction:

At the crossroads of career reinvention, one of the most challenging yet liberating aspects is the process of shedding the old and making room for the new. It's a stage where you must step back, reflect, and ask yourself: *What do I need to leave behind to fully embrace my second act?* In this chapter, we explore the profound process of unlearning outdated beliefs, letting go of ego-driven job identities, and detoxifying from toxic patterns or industries that no longer serve your evolving professional and personal goals.

This stage is about clearing the clutter—both mentally and practically—to make space for new opportunities that align with your values, passions, and a more balanced, purposeful life. It's a powerful opportunity for growth, but it requires commitment and self-awareness. In shedding what's no longer serving you, you'll be able to fully step into your second act with clarity and confidence.

Letting Go of Job Identity and Ego Attachments

For many individuals, especially those who have spent decades building their careers, a job title becomes much more than just a label— it becomes a core part of their identity. Over the years, the lines between *who you are* and *what you do* often blur, creating a powerful attachment to a role or position. This job identity can be both empowering and limiting, particularly when you reach a point in life when you no longer feel that the career you've built aligns with your evolving values or desires.

When you reach 50, the realization often dawns that you are not your job title. In fact, you are much more than the role you've inhabited for years. It's crucial to recognize that the worth you derive from your job title or corporate position is no longer a defining factor in your life. Letting go of job identity is the first step in breaking free from the ego's grip. This shift can be disorienting at first, but it's essential for reinvention. You are not defined by your career achievements; you are defined by your values, purpose, and character.

Consider Steve Jobs, who famously said, "Your work is going to fill a large part of your life, and the only way to be truly satisfied is to do what you believe is great work." Jobs himself was a perfect example of someone who let go of traditional job identities and continually reinvented himself. After being ousted from Apple, the company he founded, Jobs didn't remain attached to the title of CEO. Instead, he focused on creating new ventures (such as NeXT and Pixar) that allowed him to explore his creativity and values in new ways.

As you move toward your second act, ask yourself: *What aspects of my career have I been holding onto simply for validation or status? How much of my self-worth has been tied to external recognition, such as promotions or accolades?* These are tough questions, but they will help you dislodge the old scripts and attachments that are preventing you from moving forward.

The process of letting go of job identity involves a shift in perspective. You must recognize that your true value lies not in your professional role, but in the talents, experiences, and insights you bring to the world. Letting go of these ego attachments can be liberating—it gives you the freedom to reinvent your career, pursue new passions, and ultimately live a life that aligns more closely with your authentic self.

Identifying Toxic Patterns, Burnout Baggage, or People-Pleasing Tendencies

As you look to reinvent your career, one of the critical steps is to identify and address the toxic patterns, burnout baggage, or people-pleasing tendencies that may have been ingrained over the years. These patterns can create roadblocks to growth and change, making it difficult to move forward with clarity and confidence.

Many professionals over 50 find themselves battling *burnout*—a state of chronic stress and exhaustion that can be both physical and emotional. Burnout doesn't just affect your productivity; it chips away at your enthusiasm, passion, and sense of purpose. It often manifests as a sense of emptiness, a lack of energy, and a deep sense of dissatisfaction, despite years of hard work. For many, burnout becomes part of the identity they carry with them throughout their careers, and breaking free from it can feel like an overwhelming task.

To detox from burnout, you need to first acknowledge its presence. The longer burnout is allowed to fester, the more entrenched it becomes. Symptoms might include a sense of emotional depletion, a lack of motivation, or a disconnection from the work that once felt meaningful. You've likely spent years pushing yourself to meet deadlines, satisfy clients, or climb the corporate ladder, but now it's time to pause, reflect, and allow yourself the space to heal and redefine your approach to work.

Another common pattern is the *people-pleasing* tendency. Throughout your career, you may have prioritized the approval of others over your own needs and desires. This could have meant saying "yes" to every request, taking on too many responsibilities, or neglecting your personal boundaries to avoid conflict or disappointment. Over time, people-pleasing behaviors can lead to resentment, stress, and a lack of fulfillment in your work. It's important to recognize when your career choices are being influenced by a desire to please others rather than staying true to your own values and priorities.

To break free from these patterns, it's helpful to create clear boundaries and identify what truly matters to you in this new phase of life. Take time to reflect on the choices you've made and how they may have been driven by external expectations rather than your authentic desires. How many of your past decisions were influenced by a fear of rejection or judgment? How many of your actions were motivated by a need to please others rather than fulfill your own purpose?

Once you identify the toxic patterns that have been holding you back, you can take intentional steps to release them. This might involve seeking professional help to address burnout or working with a coach or therapist to untangle the emotional weight of people-pleasing behaviors. It's also about giving yourself permission to make decisions that prioritize your well-being, creativity, and purpose over external validation.

How to Detox from Old Industries or Toxic Work Cultures

Another important aspect of career reinvention is detoxifying from industries or work cultures that may have contributed to stress, dissatisfaction, or a sense of unfulfillment. In many cases, professionals find themselves trapped in toxic work environments or industries that no longer align with their values. These environments might involve long hours, cutthroat competition, lack of appreciation, or poor work-life balance. If your career has been built in an environment that rewards hustle culture, corporate politics, or unhealthy competition, it's important to acknowledge how those factors have impacted your well-being and sense of purpose.

Detoxing from these environments is not always easy, especially if you've invested significant time or effort in climbing the corporate ladder or achieving success in a specific industry. However, it's crucial to ask yourself: *What have I tolerated for too long that no longer serves me? What work culture, industries, or environments have I been in that drained my energy or didn't align with my values?*

Toxic work cultures often demand long hours, constant availability, and emotional labor that ultimately leads to burnout. These environments may value productivity over people, results over relationships, and performance over mental health. If you find yourself feeling depleted, unappreciated, or disconnected from your purpose, it's time to detox from those toxic systems. The process of detoxification may involve stepping away from that industry altogether or finding ways to shift your role within it. The goal is to create a work environment that aligns with your values and supports your well-being.

When considering this shift, you might find that it's necessary to explore entirely new industries or work cultures that embrace flexibility, collaboration, and holistic well-being. Whether it's nonprofit work, consulting, entrepreneurship, or remote roles in industries that emphasize sustainability or work-life balance, there are options available that align with the vision you've created for your second act.

Rituals for Letting Go: Mentally and Practically

Letting go of the old scripts, patterns, and industries that no longer serve you is not just a mental exercise—it's also a practical one. It's about creating space, both mentally and physically, for the new. To fully embrace your second act, it's essential to practice rituals that support this process of release and renewal.

Mentally, letting go begins with deep reflection. Take time to meditate, journal, or simply sit in silence to examine what you need to release in your life. This could involve reflecting on past decisions, understanding the emotional toll of toxic work environments, and processing any feelings of attachment to old roles. Writing down what no longer serves you can be a powerful exercise, as it allows you to externalize your thoughts and get a clear picture of what you need to leave behind.

Practically, letting go can involve decluttering your physical workspace, saying goodbye to outdated professional relationships, or even making a formal transition from your current role. Consider how your workspace, digital tools, or daily routines might be holding you back from embracing new opportunities. For example, you might need to update your resume, LinkedIn profile, or personal branding to reflect the new direction you're taking. It could also mean setting boundaries with clients, colleagues, or family members who might expect you to continue following old patterns.

Another practical ritual for letting go involves setting clear intentions for your second act. This could mean writing down your career vision for the future, creating a vision board, or setting specific goals for the next phase of your professional journey. By creating a tangible representation of where you want to go, you can begin to focus your energy on what's ahead rather than what's behind.

Conclusion

Letting go of the past is one of the most important—and challenging—steps in career reinvention. By unlearning outdated scripts, releasing ego-driven attachments, and detoxifying from toxic work cultures or industries, you open up the possibility for a more fulfilling and purpose-driven career. It's a process that requires reflection, self-awareness, and courage. However, it also brings incredible freedom and clarity. By shedding what no longer serves you, you make room for new opportunities that align with your evolving values and passions.

Remember, the second act is about embracing the unknown and making choices that support your overall well-being, creativity, and sense of purpose. Letting go of the old makes space for the new, and with each step, you become closer to creating a career that is not just a job but a true reflection of who you are and what you want to contribute to the world.

Chapter 5

Reinvention Options After 50

From Pivot to Passion Project

As you embark on the journey of career reinvention, the sheer number of possibilities can feel overwhelming. At 50, many professionals have accumulated a wealth of experience, knowledge, and skills, but they often feel uncertain about how to redirect those assets into something new. Fortunately, the second act of your career is filled with a variety of exciting paths that can lead to personal fulfillment, increased freedom, and financial success. The key to a successful reinvention is identifying the right path for you—one that aligns with your passions, lifestyle, and skills.

This chapter will explore several reinvention options available after 50, ranging from career shifts to entrepreneurship, freelancing, and portfolio work. Through case studies, we'll delve into the success stories of individuals who have reinvented their careers using each of these paths. Additionally, we'll explore side hustles, part-time opportunities, and remote work possibilities for those who are not yet ready to commit fully to a new venture. Finally, you'll take a quiz to help determine which reinvention path is best suited for you.

The Main Paths: Career Shift, Encore Job, Freelancing, Entrepreneurship, Portfolio Work

After 50, reinvention can take on many different forms. Whether you want to completely change industries, continue working in a more flexible capacity, or build something from scratch, the options are vast. Below, we'll break down the most common reinvention paths to help you understand the possibilities and what each option entails.

1. Career Shift: A New Path in a Different Industry or Role

One of the most common reinvention options after 50 is a complete career shift. This might involve transitioning from a long-standing role in one industry to something entirely different. Many people at this stage find that their interests, values, or priorities have changed, and they want to pursue work that feels more aligned with their evolving goals. Career shifts don't necessarily mean starting from scratch—they are often about leveraging your transferable skills and experience in new contexts.

Case Study: Sarah's Shift to Healthcare

Sarah, a seasoned marketing executive, spent over 25 years managing large-scale campaigns for tech companies. However, as she entered her 50s, Sarah began to feel a strong desire to contribute to something more meaningful. She decided to make a career shift into healthcare marketing, focusing on promoting health services for underserved communities. Although Sarah had no prior experience in healthcare, she was able to leverage her extensive marketing skills, network, and strategic thinking. After completing a certification in healthcare marketing, she transitioned into a role with a nonprofit health organization, finding both professional success and personal fulfillment.

When to Consider a Career Shift:

- You've grown tired of your current industry or job and want a fresh challenge.

- You want to align your work with your evolving personal values.

- You're willing to invest time in learning new skills or certifications.

- You want to have a greater impact or find more meaning in your work.

2. Encore Job: Returning to Work with a Fresh Perspective

An encore job is a great option for those who want to continue working but with less intensity, more flexibility, or a change of focus. It's often a scaled-back version of the role you've had before, sometimes with fewer hours, a less demanding workload, or a shift to a more fulfilling aspect of the job. Many people in their 50s opt for encore jobs when they want to remain active in the workforce but don't have the energy or desire for a full-time, high-pressure position.

Case Study: John's Encore Job in Education

John, a corporate lawyer for over 30 years, was ready for a change as he approached his 50s. He didn't want to retire, but he didn't want to continue working the grueling hours of his legal career. John decided to take an encore job teaching business law part-time at a local university.

The job allowed him to use his legal knowledge while significantly reducing the stress and time commitment of his former role. John found great satisfaction in teaching and mentoring the next generation of lawyers and is now able to balance work with personal pursuits like traveling and spending time with his family.

When to Consider an Encore Job:

- You're ready for a more flexible or less demanding work schedule.

- You want to stay engaged in a field you've worked in but at a slower pace.

- You want to give back and share your knowledge with others.

- You are nearing retirement age but don't want to fully step away from the workforce.

3. Freelancing: Building a Career Around Your Skills

Freelancing allows professionals over 50 to build a career around the skills they've developed throughout their careers without being tied to a single employer. Freelancers have the flexibility to choose their own clients, set their own hours, and work on projects that interest them. This path is especially appealing for those who want to maintain control over their work-life balance and take on projects that match their expertise.

Case Study: Linda's Freelance Writing Business

Linda, a former editor at a publishing house, transitioned to a freelance writing career after decades in the industry. Although she was initially nervous about losing the stability of a full-time job, Linda soon realized that freelancing allowed her to work on a variety of interesting projects with companies that aligned with her values. She now writes for several top-tier magazines, develops content for nonprofit organizations, and even teaches writing workshops online. Freelancing has provided Linda with the flexibility she craved, while also allowing her to continue utilizing her professional expertise.

When to Consider Freelancing:

- You have specialized skills (writing, design, programming, etc.) that are in demand.

- You prefer flexibility in your work schedule and project selection.

- You're comfortable with the uncertainty of project-based work and managing your own business.

- You're motivated by working independently and building your own brand.

4. Entrepreneurship: Starting Your Own Business or Venture

Entrepreneurship can be an exciting and rewarding path for professionals who want to build something from the ground up. Many people over 50 find that starting their own business gives them the freedom to pursue their passions, control their work environment, and contribute to their communities in meaningful ways. This can be a particularly fulfilling option for those who have always dreamed of being their own boss or want to create a business based on their personal interests.

Case Study: George's Online Retail Store

George, a former software developer, decided to launch his own e-commerce business at 55, selling specialty fitness equipment. After years of working for large tech companies, George wanted to create a business that combined his technical skills with his passion for fitness. He started small by selling products on a niche online marketplace, but as demand grew, he expanded into his own e-commerce website. Today, his online business has become successful, and George enjoys the flexibility and autonomy that comes with running his own venture.

When to Consider Entrepreneurship:

- You have a passion or idea that you want to turn into a business.

- You enjoy the idea of being your own boss and controlling your own destiny.

- You're willing to take risks and invest time and money into a new venture.

- You want the flexibility to make your own business decisions and build a company around your values.

5. Portfolio Work: Diversifying Your Projects and Income Streams

Portfolio work involves juggling multiple projects or income streams at once, allowing professionals to combine different types of work in a way that suits their interests and goals. Rather than committing to a single full-time role, portfolio workers take on part-time, contract, or consulting gigs in different areas, allowing them to build a diverse and flexible career. This is an appealing option for those who want variety and flexibility, or for those who are not yet ready to fully retire but want to reduce their workload.

Case Study: Karen's Portfolio Career

Karen, an experienced graphic designer, decided to pivot from a full-time corporate role to portfolio work. She now works with several clients on a variety of projects—ranging from branding to website design—and also offers consulting services to smaller businesses. Her portfolio career allows her to select the projects she's most passionate about while maintaining a work-life balance. Karen also enjoys the financial stability that comes from having multiple income streams rather than relying on a single employer.

When to Consider Portfolio Work:

- You have multiple skills or interests you want to pursue simultaneously.

- You want variety in your work and the flexibility to change projects.

- You're comfortable with a more fluid work schedule and managing multiple clients or projects.

- You want the flexibility to work remotely or create your own hours.

Side Hustles, Part-Time Reinvention, and Remote Work Possibilities

For those who aren't ready to fully commit to a major reinvention, side hustles, part-time roles, and remote work can be a fantastic way to ease into a new career or lifestyle. Side hustles allow you to explore new interests, build a business on the side, or supplement your income without completely leaving your current job. Part-time reinvention offers a softer transition by reducing your work hours while giving you more time to explore new ventures. Remote work opens up opportunities to work for companies globally, providing flexibility and work-life balance.

Quiz: What Reinvention Path Suits You Best?

Instructions: Answer the following questions honestly to help determine which reinvention path best suits your needs and goals.

1. What excites you most about a career change?

    o A. Learning something completely new

    o B. Having more freedom and flexibility

    o C. Working on projects that align with my expertise

    o D. Starting my own business

2. How much risk are you willing to take in your career reinvention?

    o A. I'm open to big changes and challenges

    o B. I prefer a more gradual transition

○ C. I want to maintain a balance between security and growth

○ D. I'm willing to take calculated risks if I believe in my idea

3. What type of work environment do you thrive in?

○ A. A structured environment with clear goals

○ B. A flexible and autonomous environment

○ C. A collaborative and client-facing environment

○ D. A dynamic, fast-paced environment where I'm in charge

Results:

- **Mostly A's:** Consider a Career Shift or Encore Job, where you can apply your skills to a new field or role with a reduced workload.

- **Mostly B's:** Freelancing or Portfolio Work would allow you the flexibility and variety you desire.

- **Mostly C's:** Entrepreneurship or Freelancing is a good fit for you, allowing you to build your own brand and pursue a diverse range of projects.

- **Mostly D's:** Entrepreneurship or Side Hustles may be the best path for you, giving you the freedom to build something new from the ground up.

Conclusion

The second act of your career offers a wealth of reinvention options. Whether you choose to shift to a new career, embrace a flexible encore job, become a freelancer, start your own business, or work on a diverse range of projects, the possibilities are boundless. Each of these paths has its own unique benefits, depending on your goals, values, and level of risk tolerance. By understanding these options and identifying what best aligns with your desires and skills, you can craft a fulfilling and purposeful second act that offers both professional satisfaction and personal joy.

Take time to reflect on the reinvention path that excites you most. Explore your passions, challenge outdated beliefs, and be open to new opportunities. The second act is yours to design, and with the right mindset, it can be a period of immense growth, adventure, and fulfillment.

Chapter 6

Learning New Tricks

Yes, You Can Still Upskill (Without a 4-Year Degree)

The desire to continue learning and growing doesn't end at 50—in fact, it can be the beginning of an exciting new chapter of intellectual exploration, personal growth, and career reinvention. While many might feel that their learning years are behind them, research and personal stories tell a different tale: it's never too late to upskill, explore new fields, or reinvent your career path.

In this chapter, we'll explore how the neuroscience of learning after 50 reveals that the brain can continue to adapt and form new connections. We'll look at the best online platforms and certifications designed specifically for mature learners, and we'll discuss the emotional and psychological aspects of relearning how to be a beginner, including how to let go of perfectionism and embrace the process. Lastly, we'll address the pervasive fear of tech and how to overcome the mindset that you're "too old for tech."

The Neuroscience of Learning After 50

One of the most significant barriers to learning after 50 is the belief that our brains stop being capable of adapting or changing. For decades, people believed that the brain lost its ability to create new connections after a certain age. However, neuroscience has shown that the opposite is true: neuroplasticity, the brain's ability to reorganize itself by forming new neural connections, remains powerful throughout life.

Research reveals that the older we get, the more strategic our learning becomes. Older learners are often more adept at synthesizing and making connections between information, thanks to the years of accumulated experience they've gathered. This means that even though the process of learning a new subject may take longer in your 50s than it did when you were younger, the value of that learning is often much more profound. You're able to make better use of your experience and apply new knowledge in creative ways.

This ability to continue learning is rooted in neuroplasticity. The brain remains highly adaptable, even in older age. New experiences— whether learning a new language, acquiring coding skills, or even picking up a new hobby—help create new neural pathways. These pathways not only enable you to understand the new subject matter but also keep your brain healthy, improving cognitive flexibility and memory.

As you approach learning new things after 50, it's essential to adopt a mindset that embraces the idea of life-long learning. While younger brains might have the advantage of speed in processing new information, mature brains are more adept at deeper, integrative learning, making the process itself rewarding and fulfilling.

Best Online Platforms and Certifications for Mature Learners

Learning doesn't require returning to a traditional classroom, nor does it require enrolling in a lengthy degree program. In today's digital age, there are numerous online platforms offering courses and certifications that are accessible, affordable, and perfect for mature learners who want to gain new skills at their own pace. Here are some of the best platforms to consider:

1. Coursera: Access to Top University Courses

Coursera partners with leading universities and companies to offer online courses, certifications, and even degrees in a wide variety of subjects. Many of Coursera's offerings are perfect for those looking to acquire new professional skills in a flexible learning environment.

- **Ideal for:** Learners interested in gaining certification from reputable institutions, especially in fields like data science, business, marketing, computer science, and more.

- **Recommended courses:**
  - **Google IT Support Professional Certificate**: A great starting point for those looking to break into IT or technical support without a traditional degree.

  - **Project Management Specialization**: Ideal for those looking to manage projects in any industry, from healthcare to construction.

2. Udemy: Affordable, Self-Paced Learning

Udemy is one of the largest online learning platforms, offering a vast library of courses in virtually every field imaginable. With affordable pricing and a variety of levels, Udemy is perfect for mature learners who prefer to choose their own pace and schedule.

- **Ideal for:** Beginners and intermediate learners looking for courses in technology, creative skills, business, and lifestyle development.

- **Recommended courses:**

  - **Introduction to Programming with Python**: Learn the basics of one of the most popular programming languages used in web development, data analysis, and artificial intelligence.

  - **Master Microsoft Excel**: A critical skill for those interested in business or data analysis.

3. LinkedIn Learning: Professional Development and Networking

LinkedIn Learning, formerly known as Lynda.com, offers professional development courses across business, technology, and creative industries. The advantage of LinkedIn Learning is that it integrates with your LinkedIn profile, allowing you to display completed courses and certifications directly on your profile.

- **Ideal for:** Those looking to improve their skills in business, software tools, and leadership while networking with professionals in their field.

- Recommended courses:

  - **Learning Python**: A beginner-friendly course to introduce the concepts of programming and start learning Python for web development or data science.

  - **Time Management for Leaders**: Perfect for those looking to refine their leadership skills.

4. edX: Courses from Elite Institutions

edX is another well-respected online platform offering courses from top universities such as Harvard, MIT, and Berkeley. Many courses are available for free, and certificates are available for a fee.

- **Ideal for:** Learners seeking high-quality content and academic-style courses in areas like computer science, data analysis, history, and business.

- **Recommended courses:**

  - **CS50's Introduction to Computer Science**: A comprehensive introduction to computer science, ideal for beginners who want to explore coding.

  - **Data Science for Business**: A great way to learn how to use data to make better business decisions, without needing a technical background.

5. Skillshare: Creativity-Focused Learning

Skillshare offers a wide range of courses focused on creative and entrepreneurial skills, including art, design, writing, photography, and business. It's particularly suited for those who want to develop a new hobby or business side project.

- **Ideal for:** Creative learners interested in art, graphic design, writing, entrepreneurship, or creating content.

- **Recommended courses:**
  - **Creative Writing**: For those who want to explore their creativity by learning how to write engaging stories, novels, or blogs.

  - **Designing for Non-Designers**: Perfect for anyone who wants to develop basic design skills for their business or personal brand.

Relearning How to Be a Beginner (And How to Enjoy It)

One of the most significant emotional hurdles to learning after 50 is the fear of being a beginner again. After years of experience in a particular field, the idea of starting from scratch in something new can feel intimidating. It's easy to feel vulnerable or inadequate when you're learning something unfamiliar, and it's common to experience imposter syndrome, the feeling that you don't belong in a new space.

However, embracing the beginner's mindset is one of the most powerful ways to approach new learning. The key is to accept that learning is a process, and it's okay to not know everything at the start. The joy of learning lies in the process itself—watching yourself improve, making connections, and celebrating small victories along the way.

Here are some tips for enjoying the process of relearning how to be a beginner:

- **Embrace mistakes**: Understand that mistakes are part of the learning process. They don't reflect your abilities—they're simply opportunities for growth.

- **Set small, achievable goals**: Rather than focusing on the end result, break your learning into smaller, more manageable chunks. Celebrate each milestone as a victory.

- **Stay curious**: Approach new subjects with curiosity and enthusiasm. Remember, you're not doing this because you *have to*, but because you *want to*.

- **Find a community**: Join online forums, learning groups, or workshops where you can engage with others who are also learning. Social support can make the process much more enjoyable.

Overcoming "I'm Too Old for Tech" Syndrome

One of the most common fears people have when it comes to learning new skills later in life is that technology is not for them. The idea that you're "too old" to learn something new, especially in tech, can feel overwhelming. However, this mindset is not only limiting—it's also unfounded.

Technology today is more accessible than ever, and age is no barrier to learning tech. Many successful tech professionals started their careers later in life, proving that it's possible to transition into the tech industry or integrate tech into your work, regardless of age.

Here's how to overcome the "I'm too old for tech" syndrome:

- **Start small**: Begin by learning basic digital tools that can make your daily life easier—things like email marketing, social media, or even learning how to use project management tools like Trello or Asana.

- **Take beginner courses**: As mentioned earlier, there are plenty of beginner-level courses on platforms like Coursera, Udemy, and LinkedIn Learning. Start with an introduction to programming or basic coding languages like Python.

- **Use technology for personal interests**: For example, learn to build a personal website or start a blog. These tech skills will increase your confidence while teaching you the basics of web development or content management systems.

- **Challenge your mindset**: Remind yourself that the tech world is for everyone. With consistent effort, you can build your skills just like anyone else.

Conclusion

The concept of lifelong learning is more relevant today than ever before. The idea that you can't upskill after 50, especially in technology or professional fields, is simply outdated. Your brain is more adaptable than you think, and with the right mindset, online platforms, and resources, you can build new skills and open up new professional opportunities, regardless of your age.

By embracing the neuroscience of learning, utilizing online platforms and certifications, and approaching learning with a beginner's mindset, you can expand your knowledge base, gain new qualifications, and enjoy the process of reinvention. Whether you're delving into a new tech field, learning a creative skill, or simply enriching your personal knowledge, it's never too late to start learning new tricks.

Chapter 7

Building a Brand That Fits the New You

From Résumé to Reputation

One of the most exciting and empowering aspects of career reinvention is the opportunity to reshape how the world sees you. At 50, you have accumulated a wealth of knowledge, experience, and wisdom. Now, it's time to transform this into a personal brand that reflects the evolved version of yourself—one that embraces reinvention, new passions, and a renewed sense of purpose. In this chapter, we'll explore how to build a personal brand that captures your essence after 50, how to update your résumé and LinkedIn profile, how to use storytelling to communicate your pivot, and how to age-proof your professional image with confidence.

Creating a Personal Brand After 50 That Reflects Reinvention

Personal branding isn't just for entrepreneurs or influencers—it's an essential tool for anyone navigating career changes, especially after 50. Your personal brand is the intersection of how you see yourself and how the world perceives you. In your second act, you have the unique opportunity to redefine your personal brand to match the reinvention of your career.

A personal brand that reflects your reinvention doesn't require you to abandon your past experiences; instead, it allows you to merge your past achievements with your new direction. Whether you're transitioning into a new industry, starting your own business, or even embracing a more flexible work life, your personal brand should showcase the evolution of your skills, values, and passions.

Steps to Build Your Reinvented Personal Brand:

1. **Self-Reflection**: Start by asking yourself what you truly want to communicate about your new career path. How do your past experiences, passions, and values align with the new direction you're taking? Identify the skills, strengths, and passions that are central to your reinvention.

2. **Identify Your Niche**: What sets you apart? Define what makes you unique—whether it's your experience in a particular field, your leadership style, your ability to connect with others, or your creativity. Focus on how you can position yourself as an expert or a trusted figure in your new area.

3. **Authenticity**: Authenticity is key to building a strong personal brand. Be true to yourself and communicate your journey with transparency and sincerity. Don't shy away from sharing how your past experiences inform your new path. Embrace vulnerability; it helps establish trust and connection.

Your personal brand should reflect the dynamic individual you are, not just the title you once held. This brand should align with both your professional ambitions and your personal values, making it easy for others to see who you are and what you stand for.

How to Update Your Résumé, LinkedIn, and Digital Presence

Once you have a clear understanding of your new brand, it's time to translate that into your résumé, LinkedIn profile, and digital presence. These are the key tools for conveying your reinvention to potential employers, clients, or collaborators.

Updating Your Résumé:

Your résumé is more than just a list of jobs—it's an opportunity to showcase your evolution. For those over 50, a résumé should focus on skills and achievements rather than job titles or dates. Here's how to update it effectively:

- **Focus on Transferable Skills**: Highlight the skills that are applicable to your new role or industry. Whether it's leadership, problem-solving, communication, or technical expertise, make sure your résumé showcases your transferable skills. For example, if you're shifting from corporate marketing to a consultancy role, emphasize strategic thinking, project management, and client relationship skills.

- **Showcase Results, Not Just Responsibilities**: Employers or clients want to see the impact you've made. Instead of listing job responsibilities, focus on achievements and quantifiable results. For instance, instead of saying "Managed a marketing team," say

"Led a marketing team to increase sales by 30% over the course of 12 months."

- **Highlight Continuing Education**: If you've upskilled through courses or certifications, prominently display these on your résumé. This shows your commitment to learning and adaptability, which are essential traits in any industry.

Optimizing Your LinkedIn Profile:

LinkedIn is a powerful tool for professionals over 50, and it's the first place many potential clients, partners, or employers will check. Here's how to update your profile to reflect your reinvention:

- **Update Your Headline and Summary**: Your headline should go beyond your job title and communicate your new direction. Instead of "Marketing Director," try something like "Strategic Consultant | Helping Businesses Drive Growth through Data-Driven Marketing." Your summary should reflect your journey, detailing how your experience has shaped your current focus, and what kind of value you bring to the table now.

- **Leverage Recommendations**: Ask for **recommendations** from colleagues, clients, or mentors who can speak to your evolving skills. These can be invaluable in showcasing your credibility and reinforcing your brand. Make sure to highlight your adaptability, work ethic, and achievements in the context of your reinvention.

- **Share Your Knowledge**: Post updates, articles, or thought leadership pieces related to your new field. This positions you as someone who is actively engaged in your area of reinvention and keeps your profile dynamic.

Building Your Digital Presence:

A strong digital presence is essential, regardless of whether you're seeking a new job, starting a business, or simply networking. Here's how to establish or update your digital presence:

- **Create a Personal Website or Blog**: A website gives you full control over your personal brand and allows you to showcase your portfolio, services, and personal story. It also provides a platform to display your expertise through blog posts, articles, or case studies.

- **Social Media**: Consider building a professional presence on platforms like Twitter, Instagram, or Medium, depending on your industry. Sharing insights or engaging with others in your field will reinforce your brand and help establish your reputation.

- **Consistency Across Platforms**: Ensure that your résumé, LinkedIn, website, and any other digital platforms have a consistent message that clearly communicates your reinvention and aligns with your personal brand.

Using Storytelling to Communicate Your Pivot

One of the most compelling ways to showcase your career reinvention is through storytelling. People are naturally drawn to stories because they help us relate to others, understand their journey, and connect on an emotional level. Your story of reinvention is your strongest asset when it comes to communicating the shift in your career.

Crafting Your Reinvention Story:

To tell your story effectively, focus on the following structure:

1. **The Challenge**: Start with the challenge or realization that prompted your reinvention. Perhaps you felt unfulfilled in your previous career, or you faced external factors (like a layoff) that forced you to reevaluate your path. Explain the transition in a way that people can relate to—no matter how big or small the catalyst was.

2. **The Journey**: Describe the journey you've been on to reinvent yourself. Share the steps you've taken, the skills you've learned, and the challenges you've overcome. This not only makes your story more engaging, but it also demonstrates your resilience and determination to grow.

3. **The Outcome**: End with the outcome of your reinvention— what you've gained, the new opportunities you've discovered, and how your past experiences intersect with your current role or goals. This reinforces the message that reinvention is possible at any stage of life.

Your story can be told through your résumé, LinkedIn summary, personal website, and in interviews. It's a powerful tool for showing potential employers, clients, and collaborators that you are not just a list of qualifications—you are a dynamic, evolving individual with a passion for growth.

Age-Proofing Your Professional Image with Confidence

The fear of ageism and the idea that you might be "too old" for certain roles or industries is a real concern for many professionals over 50. However, it's important to age-proof your professional image and show that you have the confidence, energy, and drive to continue excelling.

Steps to Age-Proof Your Image:

1. **Embrace Continuous Learning**: Age-proofing your brand involves showing that you're not only aware of changes in your industry but that you are actively learning and evolving. Keep up-to-date with the latest trends and technologies in your field, and let your learning efforts be visible through your digital presence.

2. **Maintain an Energetic and Positive Attitude**: Your attitude and energy are critical to age-proofing your professional image. Approach your work with passion, enthusiasm, and a positive attitude, and let this shine through in your communications and interactions.

3. **Dress for Success (and Comfort)**: While appearance is not the only factor in how people perceive you, dressing in a way that reflects your personal style and confidence is essential. As a mature professional, you don't need to adhere to outdated ideas

of what "older" workers should wear—choose attire that aligns with your personal brand and the role you are in or aspire to.

4. **Build Relationships, Not Just Skills**: In today's professional world, networking and relationship-building are often as important as technical skills. As you reinvent yourself, focus on building and maintaining relationships with people across generations, demonstrating your ability to connect with others no matter their age.

Conclusion

Building a personal brand after 50 is not only possible—it's essential. The personal brand you create will serve as your professional calling card and a reflection of your reinvention. Whether you're pivoting to a new career, starting a business, or seeking more fulfilling work, your brand should reflect who you are today—not who you were years ago.

By strategically updating your résumé, LinkedIn, and digital presence, embracing storytelling to communicate your pivot, and age-proofing your professional image, you will confidently navigate your reinvention journey. With your wealth of experience and the confidence to embrace the new you, you can create a personal brand that resonates with authenticity, passion, and expertise—ensuring your continued success and fulfillment in the second act of your career.

Chapter 8

Finding the Right Work, Not Just Any Work

Smarter Job Search and Opportunity Matching

Reinvention doesn't simply mean shifting careers or taking on new roles—it also means finding the right work that aligns with your evolving goals, values, and lifestyle. After 50, many professionals face a job market that can feel daunting, not because of a lack of experience or skills, but due to the biases and assumptions that sometimes accompany age. Finding the right job is about more than just filling a vacancy; it's about matching your skills, passions, and aspirations with opportunities that allow you to thrive in your second act.

In this chapter, we'll explore strategies for avoiding ageist traps in hiring, how to find companies that truly value your experience, and how to tap into the hidden job market through relationships and networking. Finally, we'll look at how to interview with confidence, presenting your experience with credibility instead of defensiveness. By approaching your job search smarter, not harder, you can find a role that truly fits who you are and where you want to go.

Avoiding Ageist Traps in Hiring (and How to Beat Them)

Ageism in the workplace is real. Despite the fact that many industries and companies acknowledge the value of diverse teams, age bias still persists. Whether it's the assumption that older workers lack technological proficiency, are resistant to change, or are "too expensive" to hire, ageism can present a significant challenge in your job search after 50. However, recognizing and addressing these biases head-on is the first step in overcoming them.

Recognizing Ageism in the Hiring Process:

Age discrimination can manifest in many ways during the job search process. Here are a few of the most common forms:

1. **The Job Description**: Often, job listings are written with a younger demographic in mind, using language that implies the role is suited to a certain age group. Words like "energetic," "fast-paced," or "recent graduates" can subtly signal that the employer is looking for someone younger. Even the use of certain technical jargon or a focus on skills that are tied to newer trends can make older candidates feel overlooked.

2. **Hiring Managers' Bias**: Research suggests that hiring managers may unconsciously favor younger candidates, especially if they perceive them as being "more adaptable" or "tech-savvy." Sometimes, older candidates are passed over because of a misconception that they might not fit in with a younger, more dynamic team.

3. **The Interview Process**: Ageism can become evident during interviews, where questions might not be overtly discriminatory, but are framed in a way that could suggest bias. For example, you might be asked, "How do you stay current with trends in the industry?" or "Do you feel comfortable working with a younger team?" These questions, while seemingly innocent, can put older candidates on the defensive.

How to Beat Ageism in Hiring:

1. **Emphasize Agility and Adaptability**: One of the most effective ways to overcome age bias is to counteract the stereotype that older workers are set in their ways. In your resume, LinkedIn, and interviews, emphasize your ability to adapt and stay current with new technologies, industry trends, and practices. Share examples of times you've taken the initiative to learn something new, whether it's a software program, a management technique, or a new business model.

2. **Focus on Experience as an Asset**: Your experience is one of your greatest strengths, so make sure to highlight it. Older workers are often more skilled at problem-solving, strategic thinking, and navigating complex workplace dynamics. These are invaluable traits that younger workers may not yet have developed. Frame your experience in a way that shows you can bring immediate value to the company, rather than needing a steep learning curve.

3. **Reframe Your Narrative**: When discussing your past experiences, avoid language that sounds defensive. For instance, avoid saying, "I know I'm older, but I can still learn." Instead, express your enthusiasm for the new opportunity and the insights you can bring based on your depth of experience. Reassure the interviewer that you are excited about continuing to grow in your career, and focus on what you can offer in terms of leadership, mentoring, and industry knowledge.

4. **Get Comfortable with Technology**: Overcoming the "too old for tech" stereotype requires demonstrating your tech proficiency. If you're not familiar with newer technologies, invest time in learning them. Platforms like LinkedIn Learning, Udemy, or Coursera offer a wide variety of courses that can help you stay current with tools like data analytics, project management software, and social media marketing. Certifications or online training programs can also help demonstrate your tech-savviness.

How to Find Companies That Value Experience

Not all companies are driven by age-related biases. In fact, there are many organizations that actively seek out the experience, maturity, and work ethic that older workers bring. These companies understand that older employees offer value in the form of mentorship, leadership, problem-solving, and industry insights.

Where to Find Age-Friendly Employers:

1. **Companies with Intergenerational Workforces**: Some companies actively promote a diverse workforce that includes employees from various age groups. Look for organizations that value intergenerational collaboration and have a history of employing people across different age ranges. Companies like IBM, Walmart, and Kroger are known for hiring workers from a range of ages and are committed to fostering inclusivity in the workplace.

2. **Nonprofit Organizations**: Many nonprofits value mature workers because they often bring deep industry knowledge, passion for a cause, and strong communication skills. These organizations are more likely to value experience and personal commitment over age or speed.

3. **Startups and Small Businesses**: While it's often assumed that startups only hire younger employees, many small businesses and entrepreneurial ventures welcome experienced professionals. Startups often need individuals who can manage projects, mentor teams, and help scale businesses—skills that are usually honed over years of experience.

4. **Remote Companies**: More businesses are adopting remote work models, which can offer a unique advantage for older workers who may prefer a more flexible or quieter work environment. Remote work often places less emphasis on age and more on the ability to deliver results independently. Explore

platforms like We Work Remotely or FlexJobs, which specialize in remote positions.

Researching Potential Employers:

Before you apply, do some research on the company's culture. Glassdoor, Indeed, and company websites can offer insights into how a company treats its employees, especially older workers. Look for employee testimonials that talk about diversity, workplace culture, and employee growth opportunities. This research can help you avoid companies that may have an ageist hiring culture.

Tapping into the Hidden Job Market via Relationships

Many of the best opportunities are never posted publicly. According to studies, a significant number of jobs are filled through referrals and networking rather than traditional job applications. The "hidden job market" is real, and it's one of the most powerful ways for mature job seekers to find meaningful work.

Building Relationships for Job Search Success:

1. **Leverage Your Existing Network**: If you've spent years in your industry, you likely have an extensive professional network. Start by reaching out to former colleagues, clients, mentors, and professional contacts. Let them know you're exploring new opportunities and are open to discussing potential roles. Don't just ask for a job—ask for advice, guidance, and introductions to people who can help you navigate the next phase of your career.

2. **Use LinkedIn to Connect with Industry Leaders**: LinkedIn isn't just for applying to jobs—it's also a powerful networking tool. Join groups related to your field, share your knowledge by commenting on posts, and actively reach out to thought leaders or former colleagues to set up informational interviews. A well-crafted LinkedIn profile can also attract headhunters who specialize in your field.

3. **Attend Industry Events (Virtually or In Person)**: Networking events, conferences, and trade shows are excellent ways to make connections in your industry. With the rise of virtual events, these opportunities are more accessible than ever. Whether in-person or online, attend industry events where you can meet potential employers or collaborators and learn about opportunities that aren't publicly advertised.

4. **Get Involved in Professional Organizations**: Becoming a member of industry-specific organizations or associations can offer valuable networking opportunities. Organizations like AARP's Work & Jobs section, local business chambers, or industry-specific groups (like Project Management Institute or National Speakers Association) often have job boards, events, and connections for mature workers seeking new opportunities.

Interviewing with Credibility, Not Defensiveness

The interview process is where you have the chance to showcase your value as an experienced professional, but it's also where ageism can rear its ugly head. During interviews, it's important to project confidence, credibility, and enthusiasm—not defensiveness or apology for your age. The key is to focus on the value you bring and to reframe the narrative around your experience.

How to Interview with Confidence:

1. **Be Prepared to Address Your Age Positively**: If the subject of age comes up during the interview, don't shy away from it. Instead of making excuses or apologizing for your experience, frame it as an asset. For example, you can say, "I've spent years cultivating the kind of strategic thinking and problem-solving skills that make me a great fit for this role. I've seen industry trends evolve and have adapted to those changes, which is something I'm proud of."

2. **Focus on What You Bring to the Table**: Rather than highlighting what you don't know or what might seem out of date, emphasize how your depth of experience enables you to quickly understand new challenges and solve problems. Highlight your leadership abilities, team-building skills, and your ability to mentor others. Make sure to position yourself as someone who can contribute immediately to the organization's success.

3. **Show Your Flexibility and Eagerness to Learn**: If you're shifting industries or adopting new technologies, make it clear that you are committed to learning and adapting. For example, "I have spent the past few months learning X technology, and I'm excited about applying it in my new role."

4. **Be Ready to Discuss Why You Want the Job**: Employers might be curious why someone with your experience would want to work in a new field or role. Be prepared to explain your passion for the job and how the position fits your long-term goals. This is your opportunity to highlight your enthusiasm for the work and demonstrate that your interest is genuine, not driven by necessity or convenience.

Conclusion

The process of finding the right work after 50 doesn't have to be daunting. By being strategic, overcoming age-related biases, leveraging your network, and presenting yourself with confidence, you can position yourself for success in the job market. Remember that age is not a limitation—it's an asset. Your experience, expertise, and perspective are invaluable in today's workforce. By finding companies that value what you bring, tapping into the hidden job market, and interviewing with credibility, you'll not only find work that suits you—you'll find work that excites you. With the right approach, the right opportunity is out there waiting for you to discover it.

Chapter 9

Start Something New—Even If It's Small

Turning Ideas Into Income

It's never too late to start something new, especially when it comes to pursuing a business venture or side hustle that excites you. Whether you're looking to capitalize on a passion project, use your expertise to help others, or create something that aligns with your evolving interests, midlife can be an ideal time to explore entrepreneurship. However, embarking on a business journey at this stage in life doesn't mean you need to dive into a massive startup or assume the pressure of a corporate empire. Instead, starting small, with a clear vision, is often the key to success.

In this chapter, we'll explore various business models for midlife entrepreneurs, such as consulting, coaching, and creator careers. We'll also examine microbusiness and solopreneur success stories, showing how small businesses can grow organically and sustainably. Finally, we'll provide strategies for avoiding startup overwhelm, emphasizing the importance of taking lean, manageable steps that allow you to build your business at a pace that works for you.

Business Models for Midlife Entrepreneurs

The entrepreneurial landscape has evolved over the years, and today, there are more accessible and scalable business models than ever before. Starting a business in midlife doesn't have to mean risking everything or investing a large sum of money upfront. In fact, lean business models are often the most successful, particularly for those in their 50s and beyond, who may want to test the waters before fully committing to a larger venture. Here are several business models that work well for midlife entrepreneurs:

1. Consulting: Leverage Your Expertise

Consulting is one of the most straightforward business models for professionals over 50. With decades of experience, you've likely accumulated a wealth of knowledge that can be incredibly valuable to others. Consulting allows you to monetize this expertise by helping businesses or individuals solve specific problems.

What Makes Consulting Ideal for Midlife Entrepreneurs:

- **Low Overhead**: Consulting typically requires minimal startup costs. You don't need to invest in inventory or physical storefronts; instead, you rely on your experience, knowledge, and network.

- **Flexibility**: As a consultant, you can set your own hours and work with a variety of clients, depending on your interests and availability.

- **Scalability**: Consulting businesses can be scaled by expanding your services, raising rates as your reputation grows, or hiring other consultants to work with you.

Example:

John, a former IT project manager, transitioned into a full-time consultant after retiring from his corporate job. He offers project management and technology integration consulting to small businesses looking to implement new software systems. By focusing on a niche market—small businesses that need affordable solutions—John has been able to build a successful consultancy with low overhead and a steady stream of clients.

2. Coaching: Helping Others Achieve Their Goals

Coaching is another great option for midlife entrepreneurs, especially for those with strong interpersonal skills and a passion for guiding others. As a coach, you can focus on personal development, career coaching, life transitions, or niche topics like health and wellness, leadership, or financial planning.

What Makes Coaching Ideal for Midlife Entrepreneurs:

- **Deep Reward**: Coaching allows you to directly help people achieve their personal or professional goals. This can be incredibly fulfilling, especially if you're passionate about making a difference in people's lives.

- **Low Startup Costs**: Like consulting, coaching typically doesn't require significant upfront investment. You can start by offering virtual sessions and grow your practice through referrals and word-of-mouth.

- **Variety of Niches**: Coaching can be customized to your strengths, whether it's helping others with business strategies, personal development, or even navigating career changes in midlife.

Example:

Sandy, a former HR executive, launched a career coaching business aimed at people in their 40s and 50s who are looking to pivot into new careers. Sandy helps her clients refine their résumés, improve interview skills, and find new roles that align with their passions and skills. By offering group coaching sessions, she can scale her services and reach more clients.

3. Creator Careers: Content Creation, Writing, and Media

With the rise of social media platforms, podcasts, and YouTube, content creation has become a viable business model for many entrepreneurs. If you have a passion for writing, storytelling, or creating media, becoming a content creator can be an ideal way to build a business. Content creators can earn income through advertising, sponsorships, selling products, or even offering paid memberships or subscriptions.

What Makes Content Creation Ideal for Midlife Entrepreneurs:

- **Creative Freedom**: Content creation allows you to express yourself and build a brand around your passions, whether it's cooking, travel, fitness, or lifestyle.

- **Multiple Revenue Streams**: You can monetize your content through advertising, sponsorships, product sales, affiliate marketing, and subscriptions.

- **Scalability**: As you build an audience, your content can grow and generate increasing revenue, allowing you to scale your business gradually.

Example:

Tom, a retired teacher, started a YouTube channel focused on educational content for adults who want to continue learning new skills in retirement. His channel includes tutorials, book recommendations, and life advice for people looking to reinvent themselves in their 50s and beyond. Over time, Tom has built a large following and now earns income through ad revenue, affiliate links, and online course offerings.

4. Microbusiness: Small-Scale Ventures with Low Overhead

For those looking for something more hands-on or product-based, a microbusiness can be a fantastic option. Microbusinesses are typically small-scale, low-cost ventures that are often started out of a personal interest or hobby. Whether you're making jewelry, offering handcrafted goods, or running a local service, microbusinesses allow you to test your ideas with limited financial risk.

What Makes Microbusinesses Ideal for Midlife Entrepreneurs:

- **Flexibility**: Microbusinesses allow you to be in control of your schedule and can be easily scaled or downsized based on your availability and goals.

- **Personal Fulfillment**: Microbusinesses often stem from personal passions, such as creating handmade crafts or running a small local service. This can lead to higher levels of satisfaction and joy in your work.

- **Lower Financial Risk**: Microbusinesses generally require a low startup cost, making it easier for older entrepreneurs to test the waters before fully committing.

Example:

Alice started her own customized candle business from home after she retired. She leverages her love for aromatherapy and design by creating unique candle scents and packaging. Alice sells her candles through an online store and local craft fairs. With minimal overhead and a flexible schedule, her microbusiness has grown organically, and she now makes a steady income while continuing to pursue her passion.

Microbusiness and Solopreneur Success Stories

Building a small business doesn't have to be overwhelming, and many entrepreneurs find success by starting small and scaling gradually. Let's look at some inspiring microbusiness and solopreneur success stories to show how it's possible to turn an idea into a thriving income source.

1. Rachel's Handmade Jewelry Business

Rachel, in her early 50s, decided to start her own handmade jewelry business after years of crafting jewelry as a hobby. What began as a small Etsy shop quickly gained traction due to Rachel's attention to detail and unique designs. She now sells her products through her own e-commerce site and at local craft fairs. Rachel's business has grown steadily, allowing her to support herself while indulging in a creative passion.

2. David's Freelance Graphic Design Career

David, a retired graphic designer, turned his passion for design into a freelance business. Rather than investing in a brick-and-mortar business, David offers his services remotely to small businesses, nonprofits, and entrepreneurs who need affordable design work. His microbusiness has grown through referrals, and he now has a steady stream of clients without ever needing to hire employees or invest in expensive overhead.

3. Linda's Online Wellness Coaching

Linda, who spent years working in corporate HR, used her knowledge of wellness and personal development to start an online coaching business. She provides personalized fitness plans, mindfulness coaching, and nutrition advice to clients around the world. Linda began by offering free webinars and using her social media channels to promote her services. Over time, her business has grown, and she now offers paid memberships, online courses, and one-on-one coaching.

Avoiding Startup Overwhelm with Small, Lean Steps

Starting a business in midlife can be both exciting and overwhelming. The thought of building a new business from scratch can trigger feelings of anxiety and uncertainty. However, the key to success lies in starting small and taking lean steps to get started. Instead of jumping into a large-scale startup, focus on manageable tasks and allow your business to evolve organically.

How to Start Small and Avoid Overwhelm:

1. **Define Your Minimum Viable Product (MVP)**: Start by defining the simplest version of your product or service that allows you to enter the market and begin attracting customers. This is your MVP—the core offering that you can test with real customers. For example, if you're starting a consulting business, your MVP could be a few introductory calls with clients to gauge interest and refine your approach.

2. **Create a Simple Business Plan**: Instead of a complex, detailed business plan, start with a simple one-page business plan. Outline your business idea, target audience, pricing, marketing strategies, and key financials. Having a clear plan is important, but it doesn't have to be overwhelming or rigid. Think of it as a guide rather than a blueprint set in stone.

3. **Start with Low-Cost Marketing**: When you're just starting out, marketing doesn't need to involve expensive ad campaigns. Focus on organic marketing—building relationships, creating

content, networking, and utilizing social media. Platforms like Instagram, LinkedIn, and Facebook are great tools to promote your business on a budget.

4. **Automate and Delegate as You Grow**: As your business gains traction, look for opportunities to automate tasks and delegate work. For example, use scheduling tools, email automation, and outsourcing to freelancers to free up your time and allow you to focus on high-impact activities.

Conclusion

Starting something new after 50 is not just possible—it's empowering. With the right business model, whether it's consulting, coaching, a microbusiness, or a creative venture, you can turn your ideas into income and create a career that offers both fulfillment and financial reward. Starting small and leaning into your strengths allows you to avoid overwhelm while scaling your business at your own pace. By focusing on manageable steps, embracing your experience, and staying committed to learning, you can build a business that truly aligns with your passions and goals.

Your second act is an opportunity to build something meaningful and sustainable—one small step at a time. The world is full of opportunities for midlife entrepreneurs, and now is the perfect time to take action. Start with a single idea, and watch it grow into something much larger than you ever imagined.

Chapter 10

Money Matters—Doing the Math on Reinvention

Funding the Shift Without Wrecking Your Nest Egg

The desire to reinvent yourself professionally is exciting, but it's also a big decision that involves financial considerations. After 50, many individuals are nearing retirement or are already in retirement, and the last thing anyone wants is to jeopardize their financial future while making a career shift. However, with the right planning, reinvention can not only be financially sustainable, but it can also lead to greater fulfillment and success.

In this chapter, we'll explore how to financially prepare for a career transition, how to manage risks, timelines, and income fluctuations, and how your benefits, retirement plans, and insurance coverage might be impacted by the change. We'll also cover budgeting tools and the mindset required to make a smooth, financially sound transition to your second act.

How to Financially Prepare for a Career Transition

Career transitions at any stage of life require careful financial planning, but making the leap after 50 involves additional considerations. Whether you're shifting into a new field, starting your own business, or working fewer hours in a more flexible role, it's crucial to understand how these changes will impact your finances. Fortunately, with the right preparation, you can make the transition without compromising your financial security.

1. Assess Your Financial Situation:

Before taking any significant career steps, it's essential to do a deep dive into your current financial situation. Understanding where you stand financially will allow you to make informed decisions about how much risk you can afford to take.

- **Income Sources**: Identify all your income sources, including your salary, savings, investments, and any side hustles. This will give you a clearer picture of how much you're relying on your current job to sustain your lifestyle.

- **Expenses**: Track your monthly and yearly expenses. This will help you determine how much money you need to maintain your standard of living. Consider both fixed and variable expenses, such as housing, utilities, transportation, and healthcare, as well as lifestyle costs like entertainment and dining.

- **Debt**: Assess any outstanding debts you have. It's crucial to understand how your current debt obligations may affect your ability to support yourself during your transition period. Aim to reduce high-interest debt as much as possible before making a move.

2. Calculate Your Emergency Fund:

One of the most important steps in preparing financially for a career shift is having a solid emergency fund in place. Ideally, you should have at least 6-12 months of living expenses saved before making any career transition. This fund will act as a safety net, providing you with the financial cushion you need to weather any unexpected setbacks during the transition.

- **How to Build Your Emergency Fund**: Start by setting aside a portion of your current income each month into a high-yield savings account or money market fund. If possible, try to accelerate your savings over the next year or two to build a more substantial cushion.

3. Estimate Your Income Gaps:

When you transition to a new career or start your own business, there may be a period of lower or no income. You may not immediately replace the salary you're used to, especially if you're starting a business or switching industries. Consider how long it might take to replace or increase your income from your new venture.

- **Timeline**: Establish a realistic timeline for how long it will take to ramp up your income. Factor in the learning curve, networking time, or marketing expenses if you're building a business.

- **Income Flexibility**: Consider whether you'll be able to bridge the gap with part-time work, freelance opportunities, or by drawing on other income sources, such as passive income, investment dividends, or retirement savings (if absolutely necessary).

4. Create a Financial Transition Plan:

Once you've assessed your finances and determined the level of risk you're comfortable with, you can create a financial transition plan. This plan should outline:

- How much savings you'll need to make the transition comfortably

- Any interim sources of income or part-time work you can rely on

- A timeline for when you expect to achieve financial stability in your new role

Having a clear plan will give you the confidence to move forward without feeling financially vulnerable.

Managing Risk, Timelines, and Income Dips

Career reinvention can be a risky endeavor, especially when it involves transitioning into a field you're not yet established in or starting a business. The key to success is managing that risk in a way that minimizes financial strain.

1. Managing Risk:

Risk is inherent in any career transition, but it can be mitigated through careful planning. For those who are starting their own business or taking on freelance work, the risk may seem greater. Here are a few ways to manage it:

- **Diversification**: Don't put all your eggs in one basket. Diversify your income streams to help cushion potential income dips. For instance, if you're a consultant, you might offer a combination of one-on-one services, online courses, and paid speaking engagements.

- **Gradual Transition**: If you're transitioning to a new field, consider doing so gradually. This could mean working part-time in your new role while maintaining your current job, or running your business as a side hustle before fully committing to it.

- **Side Gigs**: Consider taking on side gigs or freelance projects during your transition to keep your income consistent while you build your new career. This is a good way to test the waters and see if your new career is a sustainable source of income before you make a full-time commitment.

2. Managing Timelines:

Setting realistic timelines will help you avoid unnecessary financial strain. Keep in mind that immediate results are rare, and patience is key to a successful transition. Here are some strategies for managing your timeline:

- **Set Realistic Expectations**: When transitioning to a new career, it might take longer than expected to find a steady source of income. Be patient with yourself and avoid putting unnecessary pressure on your savings.

- **Gradual Scaling**: Focus on gradually scaling your new venture, whether it's a small business, consulting practice, or freelance gig. Instead of aiming for large profits immediately, aim for steady, incremental growth that will allow you to scale sustainably.

- **Monitor Cash Flow**: Carefully track your income and expenses during the transition period. This will allow you to spot any potential cash flow problems early, giving you time to adjust your approach if necessary.

Understanding Benefits, Retirement Plans, and Insurance Impacts

A career transition may also affect your benefits, including health insurance, retirement contributions, and other employment-based perks. Understanding these impacts is vital to ensuring that you're financially protected during your shift.

1. Health Insurance:

If you're leaving a job that provided health insurance, you'll need to find alternative coverage. Consider the following options:

- **COBRA**: If you've been working for an employer with 20 or more employees, you may be eligible for COBRA, which allows you to continue your employer-sponsored health insurance for a limited time (usually 18-36 months).

- **Marketplace Plans**: If COBRA isn't an option, explore health insurance plans through the Health Insurance Marketplace.

Depending on your income and location, you may qualify for subsidies.

- **Spouse's Plan**: If your spouse has health insurance, you may be able to join their plan, which could save you money compared to buying your own policy.

2. Retirement Plans:

When you leave a job, you have options for what to do with your retirement savings (401(k), pension, etc.):

- **Roll Over Your 401(k)**: You can roll your 401(k) into an individual retirement account (IRA) or into your new employer's retirement plan, if applicable.

- **Roth IRA or Traditional IRA**: If you're self-employed, you may want to consider contributing to a Roth IRA or a SEP IRA (for self-employed individuals). Both options allow you to continue saving for retirement while offering tax advantages.

- **Delay Retirement Draws**: If you're near retirement age and considering withdrawing from your retirement savings, try to delay withdrawals as long as possible to maximize your savings.

3. Insurance Coverage:

If you're starting a business or working as a freelancer, you may need to secure your own insurance coverage:

- **Health Insurance**: As mentioned, you'll need to find new health insurance if it's not already provided through a spouse's plan or through the government marketplace.

- **Business Insurance**: Depending on the type of business you're starting, you may need liability insurance or other forms of coverage to protect yourself and your clients.

Budgeting Tools and Mindset for Sustainable Change

In addition to careful financial planning, the right mindset is key to making your reinvention financially sustainable. Budgeting tools and a healthy approach to money will allow you to navigate your transition with confidence.

1. Budgeting Tools:

Several budgeting tools can help you track your income and expenses and ensure you're staying on track during your career shift:

- **Mint**: Mint is a popular budgeting app that allows you to link your accounts and track spending, set goals, and monitor progress.

- **YNAB (You Need a Budget)**: YNAB is designed for people who want to be more intentional with their money. It helps you prioritize your spending and create realistic budgets.

- **EveryDollar**: EveryDollar is another budgeting tool that focuses on simplicity. It helps you track income, set up a spending plan, and manage debt.

2. Mindset for Sustainable Change:

As you move through the process of reinvention, it's crucial to maintain a growth mindset. Avoid the pressure to achieve instant success, and instead, focus on long-term sustainability. Here are a few tips:

- **Patience and Persistence**: Building a new career or business takes time. Understand that setbacks are a part of the process, and don't let initial struggles deter you.

- **Balance**: Focus on balancing risk and reward. Be mindful of your financial security while also taking bold steps toward your new venture.

- **Celebrate Small Wins**: Every milestone, no matter how small, is a step forward. Celebrate your progress and use it as motivation to keep moving forward.

Conclusion

Reinventing your career after 50 is a bold and exciting endeavor, but it requires careful financial planning. By financially preparing for the transition, understanding how to manage risk and income dips, and ensuring that your benefits and insurance are covered, you can make the shift without compromising your financial future. Additionally, adopting a mindset that values patience, persistence, and sustainable change will set you up for long-term success. With the right financial preparation and a balanced approach, your career reinvention can be not only fulfilling but also financially secure.

Chapter 11

Confidence After Chaos

Rebuilding Self-Belief and Resilience

Reinvention is often born from chaos—a job loss, burnout, or a major life change that shakes your sense of security and self-worth. At this stage in life, after facing these disruptions, rebuilding your confidence and resilience may feel like an uphill battle. However, it's important to recognize that confidence can be rebuilt and that resilience is not an innate trait, but a skill that can be cultivated over time. Whether you're dealing with the aftermath of a layoff, navigating a career pivot, or simply struggling with feelings of inadequacy, this chapter is about rebuilding your self-belief and resilience after the storm.

In this chapter, we will explore how to battle imposter syndrome after a job loss or burnout, how to reframe failure and setbacks as valuable learning experiences, and how to speak your story with authority. We'll also dive into daily mental routines that will help you build self-trust and keep your confidence strong as you navigate your reinvention.

Battling Imposter Syndrome After Job Loss or Burnout

One of the most common emotional hurdles that midlife professionals face after a job loss or burnout is imposter syndrome. Imposter syndrome refers to the persistent feeling that you are fraudulent or that you don't deserve your accomplishments, despite clear evidence to the contrary. It can be particularly pervasive after a major life or career setback, such as a layoff, promotion failure, or business venture that didn't go as planned. This feeling of self-doubt can undermine your confidence, making it harder to move forward.

Understanding Imposter Syndrome:

Imposter syndrome often arises from the disconnect between how we perceive ourselves and how we believe others perceive us. When faced with a setback, such as a job loss or burnout, you may begin to internalize feelings of inadequacy. This internal dialogue often sounds like:

- *"I wasn't good enough for the job."*
- *"I'll never be able to succeed again."*
- *"I'm not cut out for this industry anymore."*

These thoughts are natural, but they are also distorted perceptions that need to be addressed. Imposter syndrome thrives on negative self-talk and perfectionism, both of which can severely hinder your ability to build confidence and resilience after a setback.

How to Battle Imposter Syndrome:

1. **Acknowledge Your Achievements**:

2. Reflect on your past successes and the skills that helped you reach them. Take stock of objective evidence of your capabilities—be it awards, positive feedback, or the concrete results of your past

work. Write these down as reminders that you deserve your success.

3. **Normalize the Feeling of Self-Doubt**:

4. Imposter syndrome is common, especially when transitioning or rebuilding after a setback. Recognize that feeling uncertain or insecure about your abilities does not mean you are incapable. In fact, many high-achieving individuals experience imposter syndrome, including successful professionals like Maya Angelou, Albert Einstein, and Sheryl Sandberg. Understanding that self-doubt is normal can help you detach from it.

5. **Reframe Your Internal Dialogue**:

6. Rather than viewing failure or setbacks as signs of incompetence, start seeing them as stepping stones to success. Acknowledge that failure is not a reflection of your worth, but a necessary part of growth. Embrace the mindset that each challenge helps you become more skilled and better equipped to handle future obstacles.

7. **Seek External Validation**:

8. Surround yourself with supportive individuals—mentors, colleagues, or peers—who can help provide an outside perspective. These people can offer insights into your strengths, accomplishments, and potential. Sometimes, an objective point of view can remind you that the negative thoughts you have about yourself are not based on reality.

Reframing Failure, Setbacks, and Rejection

At any age, failure, setbacks, and rejection are difficult to face, but when you're in the midst of career reinvention, reframing these experiences can significantly bolster your confidence and resilience. It's easy to view these experiences as personal failures, but in reality, they are often part of the necessary process for growth and success.

The Power of Reframing:

Reframing is the process of shifting your perspective on an experience or event to see it in a new, more positive light. Instead of allowing failure to define you, consider how it can reshape and strengthen you.

1. **Failure as Feedback:**

2. Instead of viewing failure as an end, consider it valuable feedback. When something doesn't go as planned, ask yourself:

   o What did I learn from this experience?

   o What can I do differently next time?

   o How can I use this lesson to approach things more strategically?

3. By treating failure as informational, you remove the emotional sting and turn it into an opportunity for learning and growth.

4. **Setbacks as Stepping Stones:**

5. Every setback brings you one step closer to your goal, even though it might not feel that way in the moment. Remember that

success rarely happens overnight. Many of the most successful entrepreneurs and professionals have faced repeated setbacks before they achieved their goals. Use the analogy of climbing a mountain: each misstep or detour might slow you down, but it doesn't mean you won't reach the summit.

6. **Rejection as Redirection**:

7. Rejection can sting, but it's also an opportunity to reassess and refine your approach. When you face rejection—whether it's a job offer, a partnership proposal, or a business venture—take a moment to reflect on the reasons behind it. Is there an aspect of your approach that needs improvement? Is this rejection steering you toward a better opportunity that aligns more with your goals? By seeing rejection as redirection, you can channel the energy you've invested into something more aligned with your long-term vision.

8. **Gratitude for the Journey**:

9. The process of reinvention is messy and unpredictable, but it's also the process of learning and becoming. Embrace the fact that setbacks and rejection have added depth to your character and resilience. Gratitude can help shift your mindset from one of frustration to one of appreciation for the journey itself.

How to Speak Your Story with Authority

As you rebuild your confidence and continue your reinvention, being able to speak your story with authority is crucial. Whether you're sharing your experience in an interview, at a networking event, or in casual conversations, your story is a powerful tool that communicates your value and resilience.

1. Own Your Narrative:

Your story is yours to tell, and how you choose to frame it will dictate how others perceive you. Own your experiences—don't shy away from talking about challenges you've faced. Instead, present them as pivotal moments that contributed to your growth. Speak with pride about how you've handled difficulties and how they've shaped your strengths.

2. Be Authentic:

When speaking about your experiences, be authentic and honest. Share both your successes and your struggles. Vulnerability fosters connection, and when you allow others to see the human side of your story, they will respect and relate to you more deeply. Speak confidently about what you've learned from each experience, whether it was a triumph or a failure.

3. Focus on Strengths and Solutions:

While it's important to acknowledge struggles, it's equally important to focus on how you've overcome them. Share the specific skills, insights, and strategies you used to handle challenges. This demonstrates resilience and problem-solving ability, key qualities that employers and collaborators are looking for.

4. Keep It Positive:

Make sure that when you speak about your reinvention, the tone is positive and forward-focused. Don't dwell on past failures; instead, show how you're using your past experiences as a springboard for the future. Position yourself as someone who is actively seeking new opportunities and ready to contribute.

Daily Mental Routines to Build Self-Trust

Building self-belief and resilience requires consistent effort—it doesn't happen overnight. Establishing daily mental routines can help you stay focused, positive, and confident as you continue your reinvention journey. Here are some mental routines that can help you stay on track:

1. Morning Mindset Ritual:

Start your day with a positive mindset by practicing gratitude and intention-setting. Take a few minutes every morning to write down what you're grateful for and identify one goal or intention for the day. This helps set a positive tone and gives you a clear focus.

2. Affirmations and Visualization:

Use affirmations to remind yourself of your strengths and capabilities. Stand in front of the mirror and affirm statements like:

- "I am capable of achieving my goals."

- "I have the skills and resilience to overcome any challenge."

- "I am worthy of success and happiness."

Combine affirmations with visualization. Picture yourself succeeding in your new career or business, feeling confident and fulfilled. Visualization is a powerful tool that aligns your thoughts and actions toward your goals.

3. Reframe Negative Thoughts:

Whenever you notice negative or self-doubting thoughts, make it a habit to reframe them. For example, if you catch yourself thinking, "I'm too old to learn new skills," counteract it by saying, "I have decades of experience that I can build on to learn new things." This will help you shift your mindset and regain confidence in your abilities.

4. Daily Reflection:

Take time at the end of each day to reflect on your accomplishments, no matter how small. Celebrate your wins and think about how you've grown throughout the day. This helps build self-trust and reinforces the belief that you are progressing toward your goals.

Conclusion

Rebuilding confidence and resilience after a setback or career disruption is not easy, but it's absolutely possible. By battling imposter syndrome, reframing failure and setbacks, and speaking your story with authority, you can regain control of your narrative and move forward with confidence. Establishing daily mental routines focused on self-belief and gratitude will allow you to keep building the resilience needed to tackle challenges, adapt to new opportunities, and ultimately succeed in your reinvention.

Remember: You've already overcome challenges in your life, and now it's time to use those experiences as a foundation for your next chapter. With the right mindset and daily commitment, you can rebuild your confidence and approach your reinvention journey with strength, optimism, and resilience.

Chapter 12

The Reinvention Lifestyle

Designing Work That Feeds, Not Drains You

The world is changing faster than we could have ever imagined. The pace of technology, global connectivity, and shifts in societal values are all creating new ways of living, working, and thriving. In this rapidly evolving landscape, many men are finding themselves at a crossroads—tired of the daily grind, disillusioned by traditional career paths, and searching for more meaningful ways to live and work. The question arises: how can you create a lifestyle that feeds you—one that aligns with your passions, nurtures your relationships, and leaves you feeling energized rather than drained?

This chapter is for those who are ready to reinvent their approach to work and life. It's for those who want to break free from the old model of success that emphasizes burnout and sacrifice and instead design a life that is sustainable, fulfilling, and authentic. Reinventing your lifestyle means redefining what work and success look like for you—not as something that takes away from your life, but something that nourishes you and propels you forward.

In this chapter, we will explore how to design a life that works for you, by focusing on the crucial elements of time, energy, and boundary management. You will learn how to integrate your work with wellness, relationships, and joy—creating systems that support, not sabotage, your goals. We will dive into practical tools and rituals for the next decade, helping you build the foundation for a life that is balanced, purposeful, and invigorating.

Let's begin the journey of creating the "Reinvention Lifestyle"—a life where work is a source of fulfillment, not stress, and where every day contributes to your broader goals of well-being and personal success.

Time, Energy, and Boundary Management for Your Second Shot

At the heart of the reinvention lifestyle is a profound understanding of time, energy, and boundaries. For too long, men have been conditioned to view time as a scarce resource—something to be fought over, managed under duress, and often sacrificed for productivity and achievement. The result? A never-ending cycle of exhaustion, burnout, and dissatisfaction.

But time is not the only resource we need to manage. Energy—our physical, emotional, and mental reserves—is just as important, if not more so. Many of us push through our days, neglecting our bodies, minds, and hearts in the name of success, only to find ourselves drained and unmotivated by the end of it all. A reinvention lifestyle acknowledges the need for a sustainable balance between time, energy, and well-being. It's about designing a schedule and a system that supports the optimal use of both.

1. Time Management: Prioritization, Not Perfection

To truly reinvent your lifestyle, you need to become a master of prioritizing time—not overloading yourself with endless tasks or obligations. Time management is not about doing more; it's about doing the right things with the time you have. Instead of striving to "fit it all in," start by identifying what truly matters to you.

- **Defining Your Big Three**: Each day, identify three key tasks or areas of focus that align with your long-term vision. These tasks should serve your most important goals, whether it's building your career, investing in your relationships, or focusing on your personal well-being. By narrowing your focus, you ensure that your time is used effectively.

- **The 80/20 Rule (Pareto Principle)**: Use the Pareto Principle to focus on the 20% of activities that will give you 80% of your desired results. For example, if you're an entrepreneur, focus on the core activities that drive revenue and growth—sales, product development, and customer satisfaction. Leave less important tasks—like responding to non-urgent emails or checking social media—until later in the day or week.

- **Time Blocking**: Use time blocking to set specific periods for focused work, breaks, and personal time. This prevents the all-too-common trap of "work bleeding into personal time" and ensures you have a structure that fosters focus and productivity. Make sure to include time for rest, meals, and relaxation, so that you can recharge your energy reserves throughout the day.

2. Energy Management: The Key to Sustainability

Energy is the fuel that powers your life. Unlike time, which is finite and often outside of our control, energy is something that can be cultivated, managed, and replenished. When you're managing your energy, you're optimizing your capacity to do the things that matter most in life, without feeling drained.

- **Physical Energy**: The most obvious and essential aspect of energy management is physical health. Exercise, sleep, and nutrition directly impact how we feel and perform. Whether it's starting your day with a morning workout, taking short walks throughout the day, or prioritizing seven to eight hours of quality sleep, these habits ensure that you have the physical energy to tackle your work and personal life with vitality.

- **Mental Energy**: Mental energy refers to your cognitive capacity to focus, problem-solve, and make decisions. When you're mentally fatigued, everything becomes harder—from creative thinking to simple tasks. To preserve mental energy, it's crucial to practice mindfulness, take regular breaks, and engage in activities that recharge your brain, like reading, journaling, or meditating.

- **Emotional Energy**: Emotional energy often goes overlooked, but it's just as important. Negative emotions—such as stress, anger, or frustration—consume our energy reserves, leaving us feeling burnt out. To manage emotional energy, it's important to recognize your emotions without judgment, and practice techniques such as deep breathing, mindfulness, and self-compassion. Engaging in fulfilling relationships and activities that bring you joy also replenishes emotional energy.

3. Boundary Management: Saying No to Say Yes

The ability to set boundaries is a key part of living the reinvention lifestyle. When you design a life that feeds you, you must recognize when you're spreading yourself too thin or allowing outside forces to encroach on your time and energy. The most successful and fulfilled individuals are those who have learned to say "no" to distractions and commitments that don't align with their values and goals.

- **Work-Life Boundaries**: In today's digital world, work can follow us everywhere. Setting clear work-life boundaries is essential to ensuring you don't burn out or lose sight of what's important. Designate specific hours for work and others for personal time, and communicate these boundaries to colleagues, clients, and family. When you're off the clock, make sure you actually *are* off the clock.

- **Personal Boundaries**: Your energy is precious, and it's important to protect it. Whether it's limiting time spent with draining people, avoiding negative influences, or saying no to activities that don't serve you, setting boundaries around your personal life is crucial. Be intentional with where and how you invest your time, and make sure that your energy is spent in ways that align with your values and goals.

- **Technology Boundaries**: Technology can be one of the most distracting forces in our lives. Set specific boundaries for checking emails, social media, and notifications. Use apps to limit screen time or designate tech-free zones, such as during meals or before bed. By setting these boundaries, you'll preserve your mental energy and maintain a healthier relationship with your devices.

Integrating Work, Wellness, Relationships, and Joy

A reinvention lifestyle doesn't focus on work alone—it's about achieving balance between all areas of your life: work, wellness, relationships, and joy. When you integrate these aspects seamlessly, they create a life that is fulfilling, sustainable, and aligned with your values.

1. **Work and Wellness Integration**: Instead of separating your work life from your well-being, find ways to integrate them. This might mean building wellness practices into your workday, such as stretching breaks, mindful breathing exercises, or regular walks outside. When you prioritize your physical and mental health as part of your work routine, you're setting yourself up for success both professionally and personally.

   o **Wellness Breaks During Work**: Schedule breaks during your workday where you step away from the computer or desk. Use this time for a quick walk, some stretches, or even meditation. This gives you a mental reset and helps maintain your focus and productivity for the rest of the day.

2. **Relationships and Joy**: Strong relationships are a cornerstone of a fulfilling life. Make sure that you are investing time and energy into the people who matter most to you—family, friends, and your community. Also, prioritize activities that bring you joy and allow you to relax. The idea is to create a life where work does not overshadow your personal connections and passions.

   o **Quality Time Over Quantity**: It's not about how much time you spend with loved ones, but how you spend it. Make sure that when you're with people, you're fully present, engaged, and supportive. Similarly, spend time doing things that make you happy, whether it's a hobby, exercise, or pursuing a passion project. These moments of joy replenish your emotional energy and keep you motivated.

Creating Systems That Support, Not Sabotage, Your Goals

To build a reinvention lifestyle that lasts, you need to create systems that support your well-being and goals—not hinder them. These systems will help you stay focused, maintain balance, and keep your priorities in check. A system is a framework that automates the habits and practices that align with your values and goals, so you don't have to think about them constantly.

1. **Daily Systems**: Create small, manageable systems that ensure your daily routines support your well-being. This could be a morning routine that involves exercise, journaling, and planning

your day. Or an evening routine that helps you wind down with relaxation techniques, reading, or meditation. These daily rituals set the tone for your day and reinforce your goals.

2. **Weekly and Monthly Systems**: Set aside time each week to reflect on your goals, track your progress, and plan for the upcoming week. Every month, take a moment to review your accomplishments, recalibrate, and adjust your plans as necessary. These systems keep you on track without overwhelming you with constant decision-making.

3. **Automating Tasks**: Find ways to automate tasks that don't require your personal touch. This could include meal prepping, using technology to manage your schedule, or setting up automatic bill payments. When routine tasks are automated, you free up mental and emotional energy to focus on what truly matters.

Lifestyle Design Tools and Rituals for the Next Decade

As you look ahead to the next decade, think about what kind of life you want to create for yourself. What legacy do you want to leave? What kind of work, wellness, and relationships will bring you joy? By designing your lifestyle intentionally, you can ensure that your future is aligned with your values and goals.

1. **Vision Board**: Create a vision board or journal to visualize the life you want to lead. Include your career goals, personal

aspirations, wellness targets, and relationship priorities. Refer back to this board regularly to keep your goals front and center.

2. **The Power of Reflection**: Make reflection a central part of your lifestyle. Regularly assess where you are in relation to your goals, what habits are working, and what needs to be adjusted. This constant feedback loop will allow you to refine your systems and stay aligned with your evolving vision.

Conclusion:

Designing a life that feeds, rather than drains, you is within your reach. By managing time, energy, and boundaries, you can create a sustainable lifestyle that balances work, wellness, relationships, and joy. The reinvention lifestyle isn't about perfection; it's about creating systems and rituals that support your goals and allow you to live in alignment with your true self.

As you step into the next decade of your life, take the lessons from this chapter to heart: integrate your work with wellness, nurture relationships that matter, prioritize joy, and build the systems that will support your personal evolution. The future is yours to design. Let it be a life that fuels you, not drains you.

Chapter 13

Leaving a Legacy, Not Just a Job

Meaning, Mentorship, and Making a Mark

As you approach the later stages of your career or embark on a new venture, it's natural to consider what kind of legacy you want to leave behind. After decades of hard work, the question arises: *What's the greater purpose of this next chapter?* Is it about money, status, or recognition? Or is it about something deeper—creating lasting impact, mentorship, and meaning?

This chapter is about thinking beyond the job itself and contemplating the legacy you want to leave—not just for your family or immediate circle, but for the world at large. Whether you're focused on helping others through mentorship, contributing your wisdom through volunteering, or creating a platform for thought leadership, there are countless ways to make your second shot count—for yourself and others.

We'll explore how you can create value through mentoring, volunteering, and thought leadership, and how to find the impact that resonates with your deeper values. We'll also reflect on how you can build a legacy that aligns with the life you want to live—a life that's meaningful not just for you, but for the people who will follow in your footsteps.

Beyond Money: What Impact Do You Want to Leave?

At a certain point in your career, the traditional drivers of success—money, titles, and accolades—lose their luster. These things may have been motivating in the past, but as you reach a later stage in life, the question of impact begins to take precedence. After all, money isn't everything, especially when you've already achieved a certain level of financial security. The real question becomes: *What do you want to leave behind?*

The Shift from Wealth to Impact

While financial success is often a necessary part of career growth, many professionals over 50 begin to realize that legacy is about more than just monetary gain. The desire to contribute to society, to help others, and to create lasting value becomes a more powerful motivator. In the second act of life, it's about creating something of meaning, something that will outlast your career and continue to have a positive impact long after you've moved on from your professional life.

Ask yourself:

- *What is the lasting mark I want to leave on the world?*

- *What kind of values do I want to be remembered for?*

- *What causes or initiatives matter most to me now?*

Your legacy might be about creating opportunities for others—whether through career mentorship, charitable giving, or starting a business that solves important problems. It could also be about sharing wisdom and making the world better through thought leadership.

Perhaps your legacy will be rooted in the creation of a community or the development of new ideas that push society forward in a meaningful way.

Legacy Beyond Career Achievements

Consider professionals like Oprah Winfrey, who built a multi-billion-dollar empire, but whose true legacy comes from the powerful conversations she facilitated, the lives she inspired, and the social impact she created. Similarly, Warren Buffet, though famous for his wealth, speaks often about the impact of his investments in philanthropic causes and the importance of giving back. These individuals show us that true legacy is about more than the wealth or titles one accumulates—it's about the lasting impact made on others and the world.

In your case, it's about deciding where to channel your energy and expertise to create a legacy of significance—one that reflects your values, passions, and the change you want to see in the world.

Creating Value Through Mentoring, Volunteering, or Thought Leadership

One of the most powerful ways to leave a lasting impact is by investing in others. Whether it's through mentoring, volunteering, or thought leadership, these avenues allow you to share your experience, offer guidance, and influence future generations.

Mentoring: Sharing Knowledge and Experience

Mentoring is one of the most rewarding ways to give back to the professional community. By mentoring others, you can help guide someone's career, provide insight into the challenges they may face, and pass down wisdom that can shape their success. Mentorship doesn't just benefit the mentee—it can also reinforce your own learning, create valuable connections, and provide personal satisfaction as you see someone else grow and thrive.

- **How to Be an Effective Mentor:**

- Being a mentor requires more than just offering advice. It's about actively listening, being patient, and offering support based on the unique needs of your mentee. As you engage in mentorship, focus on nurturing confidence, helping your mentees develop their skills, and encouraging them to take on challenges and push beyond their comfort zones.

- **Formal Mentoring Programs:**

- Many organizations, especially in industries like tech, education, and healthcare, offer formal mentoring programs that match experienced professionals with younger, less experienced individuals. If you're not sure where to begin, look for these programs through industry associations or community groups.

Volunteering: Making an Impact on the Ground Level

Volunteering is another impactful way to leave a legacy. Whether you're giving your time to a cause that resonates with you, or sharing your professional expertise with nonprofits or community groups, volunteering allows you to give back to your community in a meaningful way. It also offers a sense of purpose and connection that can be incredibly fulfilling.

- **Volunteer Opportunities:**

- Many nonprofits, charities, and community organizations rely heavily on volunteers to fulfill their missions. This can include everything from coaching youth sports teams to providing career counseling for underserved communities, to helping with event planning or fundraising for organizations in need.

- **Volunteering for Impact:**

- Think about where your experience can truly make a difference. If you've spent your career in business, you may be able to help a nonprofit with strategic planning, or if you have a background in healthcare, you might volunteer your services in clinics or educational settings.

Thought Leadership: Sharing Your Wisdom

Becoming a thought leader means sharing your knowledge and expertise with a wider audience, whether through writing, speaking, or creating content. Thought leaders influence industries, shape conversations, and leave a legacy of ideas that continue to impact the world long after their initial dissemination.

- **Writing and Publishing:**

- You can write books, articles, or blogs about the lessons you've learned throughout your career. Sharing your insights allows others to benefit from your experiences and adopt strategies that have proven effective over time.

- **Public Speaking and Podcasting:**

- Speaking at conferences, giving seminars, or hosting podcasts allows you to build an audience and create a platform where you can inspire others. Sharing stories about your journey, your challenges, and your successes helps to elevate your influence and encourages others to learn from your path.

- **Creating Educational Content:**

- If you've honed specific skills over the years, consider creating courses or workshops that teach others in your field. This provides an avenue for others to benefit from your knowledge, while also establishing you as a credible voice in your industry.

Making Your Second Shot Count—For Yourself and Others

Your second shot is about more than just securing another job or career. It's about designing a life that is fulfilling, meaningful, and impactful. As you transition into the next phase of your career, make sure you're doing it with the intention of leaving a mark that reflects your true values.

Creating Purposeful Work

Consider what you're passionate about and how you can align your new career or business with these passions. Your second act should be more than just a way to earn income—it should be an opportunity to fulfill your purpose and create a legacy that reflects the kind of impact you want to leave.

- **Be Intentional**: Take time to reflect on how your next career step can align with your values. What do you want to contribute to the world? How can your skills and experience shape others' lives?

- **Pursue Meaningful Projects**: Look for projects that give you a sense of purpose. Whether it's volunteering, mentoring, or launching a cause-driven business, these initiatives often provide greater fulfillment than simply pursuing profit.

Building a Sustainable Legacy

Building a legacy doesn't require grand gestures. Even small actions—like offering mentorship, writing a book, or dedicating time to a cause you care about—can create ripple effects that last for generations. Keep in mind that your legacy doesn't have to be perfect, it just has to be authentic to who you are and the change you want to see in the world.

Final Reflections: Better Aim, Better Life

As you move forward in your second act, remember that your legacy is a reflection of the choices you make, the impact you create, and the values you uphold. This chapter of your life is about meaning—not just money or accolades, but the value you create through your work, your interactions, and your contributions to others. Whether through mentoring, volunteering, or thought leadership, you have the opportunity to make a lasting mark.

Reinvention is not just about the work you do; it's about the life you lead. By focusing on purpose, impact, and legacy, you can build a second act that's more fulfilling, meaningful, and ultimately more rewarding for both you and those around you. Your second shot is an opportunity to leave a legacy of significance—one that reflects who you are, what you stand for, and the change you want to inspire in the world.

Conclusion: As you stand on the threshold of a new chapter—whether it's retirement, a career shift, or a renewed calling—the idea of leaving behind more than just a job title becomes deeply personal and profoundly important. Chapter 13 reminds us that the culmination of a career is not defined by income, status, or accolades, but by the impact we make on others and the values we choose to embody.

Legacy is not about grandeur; it's about intentionality. It's about asking the hard questions: *What will I be remembered for? Who did I lift up? What changes did I contribute to?* When you realign your focus from wealth to impact, your efforts become more fulfilling and meaningful. Through mentoring, you pass the torch to the next generation. Through volunteering, you enrich communities with your presence and experience. Through thought leadership, you spark new conversations and shape the future of your field.

This chapter also reinforces that creating a legacy doesn't require monumental actions. Small, consistent contributions—whether it's guiding a young professional, writing about your journey, or offering your expertise to causes you care about—can create ripples that extend far beyond your immediate circle.

Your second shot is your chance to not only reinvent your work but to enrich your life. It's a time to create purpose-driven goals, pursue meaningful projects, and lead with authenticity. By anchoring your legacy in mentorship, service, and wisdom-sharing, you ensure that your influence will live on—not just in the results of your work, but in the lives you've touched. In the end, the most rewarding legacy is one that reflects your deepest values and inspires others to build upon the path you've paved.

Bonus Materials: Your Tools for Reinvention

As we wrap up the core journey of career reinvention and legacy-building, it's time to shift our focus to what I call the "gear kit" for your second shot. You've explored the philosophies and frameworks that drive meaningful reinvention; now, it's time to roll up your sleeves and get practical. This chapter isn't just a wrap-up—it's your launchpad. It contains tools, resources, and self-reflective instruments designed to help you act on everything you've learned.

Whether you're on the verge of a career shift, building a new identity, or refining your legacy, these materials will guide you beyond theoretical insights into actionable outcomes. Consider this chapter your companion pack: ready to be used, customized, and returned to whenever needed.

Let's break down each of these resources, not just in terms of what they are, but how to use them strategically.

Reinvention Roadmap Worksheet: Charting Your Path with Clarity

Most people don't lack ideas—they lack structure. The Reinvention Roadmap Worksheet is a strategic tool designed to help you connect the dots between your experiences, aspirations, and opportunities. Think of it as your blueprint for the next phase of your professional life.

What It Does

This worksheet helps you:

- Reflect on your career history—achievements, setbacks, lessons.

- Identify core values and passions that matter most to you now.

- Map out potential career or contribution paths aligned with your current lifestyle goals.

- Define what reinvention looks like for you personally.

How to Use It

This is not a worksheet you race through in one sitting. It's best approached as a reflective exercise over a few sessions. Start by reviewing your professional timeline. Jot down not only your positions and milestones but also the emotions, motivations, and shifts behind them. What patterns do you see?

Then move into values alignment. Use this section to cross-examine what genuinely lights you up. Many people over 50 find that what once motivated them—climbing the corporate ladder, earning big bonuses—

no longer holds the same sway. If your inner compass has shifted, that's perfectly natural. Let this worksheet be your recalibration tool.

Finally, move into vision casting. Sketch out what the next 5, 10, or even 15 years could look like—not just career-wise, but holistically. Where do career, legacy, personal life, and contribution overlap? That intersection is where your second shot finds its most fertile ground.

Pro Tip

Revisit this worksheet quarterly. It's not a static document. As you test, experiment, and evolve, so will your map. Let it adapt with you.

"Second Shot" Case Study Vault: Learning from Real Lives in Reinvention

There's nothing quite like seeing your own possibilities mirrored in someone else's transformation story. The "Second Shot" Case Study Vault features a collection of real-world reinvention journeys— individuals over 50 who radically shifted gears, rekindled dormant dreams, or found entirely new missions in life. These are not celebrities or outliers. These are real people, just like you, who navigated uncertainty with courage, clarity, and commitment.

What It Includes

- Professionals who transitioned from corporate roles into passion-driven entrepreneurship.

- Retirees who found purpose in volunteering, mentoring, or community-building.

- Individuals who reinvented themselves through academia, the arts, or activism.

- Caregivers and parents rediscovering personal identity through late-stage career pivots.

Each case study is carefully curated with:

- A snapshot of where they started.

- The inflection point that triggered change.

- The emotional and logistical challenges they faced.

- Strategies and tools that helped them pivot.

- Where they are now—and how they define success today.

Why It Matters

Reading about reinvention isn't the same as watching it unfold in real lives. These case studies bridge that gap. They show you that it's never too late to change, and more importantly, that change doesn't have to look like starting from scratch. Sometimes it's a refinement. Sometimes it's a leap. But in every case, there's proof that reinvention is not only possible—it's often the most authentic stage of one's career.

How to Apply It

Use these stories as mirrors. Identify which stories resonate most with your current stage or aspirations. Reflect on the mindset shifts, strategies, and support systems these individuals leveraged. What parallels can you draw in your own journey?

Then go one step further—reach out. Some of these case studies include professional links or social platforms. Connection is part of reinvention. Build your new network around those walking similar paths.

Age 50+ Career Reinvention Resources List: Your Personal Toolkit

Information is not wisdom, but it is a crucial starting point. The Reinvention Resources List is your personal toolbox of hand-picked recommendations tailored for career shifters and legacy-builders over 50.

What's Inside

- **Books** on second-act careers, personal reinvention, thought leadership, and mindset transformation.

- **Online courses** from platforms like Coursera, LinkedIn Learning, and edX, tailored to midlife learners.

- **Coaching and mentoring directories** that specialize in late-career professionals.

- **Communities and forums** where reinvention-minded individuals gather to share, support, and collaborate.

- **Nonprofit and volunteering platforms** ideal for professionals looking to contribute time and expertise meaningfully.

- **Startup incubators and pitch labs** open to mature entrepreneurs.

- **Job boards** specifically geared toward experienced professionals (e.g., Encore.org, The Muse, FlexJobs, and RetiredBrains).

Why This Matters

When beginning a new chapter, it's easy to feel like an outsider in a world dominated by younger, tech-savvy professionals. This resources list counters that perception by offering avenues curated specifically for your stage, strengths, and style. These aren't generic tips—they are targeted, vetted, and valuable.

How to Use It

Start with your most immediate goal. If you're considering entrepreneurship, head to the startup incubator section. If you're exploring impact work, browse the volunteering platforms. Bookmark what resonates, experiment with new tools, and build momentum one resource at a time.

Set a goal: Explore at least two new resources each month. The more you engage with new platforms, the broader your reinvention playground becomes.

Self-Assessment Quiz: "What's Next for Me?"

Too many people stall in reinvention because they don't know where to begin. They're overwhelmed by options, fearful of making the wrong move, or unsure of what truly aligns with their evolving identity. The "What's Next for Me?" Self-Assessment Quiz helps cut through that noise. It's designed to get you introspective, honest, and excited about possibilities.

What It Measures

- **Values and Motivators:** What drives you now, and how has that changed?

- **Strengths and Transferable Skills:** What do you bring to the table that's relevant across industries or initiatives?

- **Lifestyle Goals:** Are you seeking full-time work, part-time engagement, volunteerism, or a sabbatical?

- **Risk Tolerance:** Are you comfortable launching a startup, or do you prefer established systems and roles?

- **Preferred Legacy Tracks:** Do you see yourself as a mentor, creator, supporter, or disruptor?

How It Works

The quiz includes a combination of reflective prompts, scaled response options, and scenario-based choices. Once completed, it generates a profile with:

- A breakdown of your dominant reinvention style (e.g., "The Builder," "The Sage," "The Explorer," "The Guide").

- A tailored list of career paths, impact projects, or reinvention models suited to your profile.

- Actionable next steps to begin exploring each path.

Why It Works

We often think we know ourselves—until we're asked the right questions. This quiz brings clarity where there was confusion. It doesn't hand you all the answers, but it certainly provides the right questions to begin crafting a future that's informed and intentional.

A Word of Encouragement

There's no "perfect" reinvention path. There's only alignment. This quiz is a tool to help you narrow down the landscape and spotlight the paths most in sync with your skills, values, and lifestyle.

Integrating the Bonus Materials into Your Journey

These bonus materials are not "extras"—they are essential building blocks for action. Throughout this book, we've explored mindset, meaning, motivation, and movement. But now, we get tactical. Use these tools as you would a compass and a journal: to navigate and to record. To orient yourself and to measure progress.

How to Get the Most Out of These Materials

- **Set a dedicated reinvention hour** each week to use one or more of these tools.

- **Involve trusted peers or mentors** in your process—share your roadmap, discuss your quiz results, reflect together on case studies.

- **Create a progress log.** Keep track of where you started and what you're discovering.

- **Give yourself deadlines.** Reinvention doesn't have to be rushed, but it does require forward motion.

Epilogue

These materials were not designed to sit in a folder or gather digital dust. They are interactive. Alive. Meant to spark thought, guide discovery, and fuel action. But like any tool, their value lies in how and when you use them.

This isn't homework—it's homebuilding. You are building the next home for your talents, time, and energy. The second shot isn't just a do-over. It's a do-better. A do-braver. A do-more-aligned-with-who-you've-become.

Take these materials and make them yours. Scribble in the margins. Highlight what hits home. Revisit often. Because reinvention, after all, is not a one-time act. It's a life-long muscle. These tools are here to help you keep that muscle strong, flexible, and ready for whatever comes next.

So now, with clarity in your heart and strategy in your hands, the only question left is:

Are you ready to begin your second shot?

www.ingramcontent.com/pod-product-compliance
Lightning Source LLC
Chambersburg PA
CBHW070121030426
42335CB00016B/2228